SASQUATCH

TRUE-LIFE ENCOUNTERS WITH LEGENDARY APE-MEN

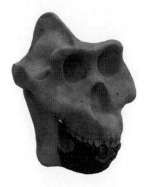

RUPERT MATTHEWS

CHARTWELL
BOOKS, INC.

This edition printed in 2008 by
CHARTWELL BOOKS, INC.
A Division of **BOOK SALES, INC.**
114 Northfield Avenue
Edison, New Jersey 08837

Copyright © 2008 Arcturus Publishing Limited
26/27 Bickels Yard, 151–153 Bermondsey Street,
London SE1 3HA

ISBN-13: 978-0-7858-2383-4
ISBN-10: 0-7858-2383-2

Printed in China

CONTENTS

YETI   MARICOXI   WILDMAN

Introduction

If we are to take the reports at face value it would seem that gigantic upright hominid apes are stomping around North America in large numbers. They are said to steal food from camp sites, attack cars and leer through bedroom windows. According to some accounts they might run off as soon as a human approaches, but it seems that they are just as likely to kidnap hapless intruders and force them to live in the forests for months on end. They are also reputed to smell terrible. These creatures are called Bigfoot or Sasquatch.

Hominid apes have also been seen wandering the jungles of South America, although they appear to be smaller and less human-like than those of the north. However, it is not just in the Americas that these apes are to be found. The high Himalayas are home to the enigmatic Yeti, the Sumatran jungles harbour a short hairy man called the Orang Pendek and Central Asia is stalked by a being that might be a primitive form of human, which locals call the Almas. Over the border in China, reports are made of an almost identical beast called the Yeren while even Australia gets in on the act with a big hairy ape called the Yowie.

What all of these animals, or perhaps humans, have in common is that conventional science does not recognize their existence, so they are classed as 'cryptids' or 'hidden ones'. That is, sightings have been reported but there is not enough evidence to satisfy the scientific community. The standard of evidence needed is high. Each of these creatures will be seen as a cryptid until an example – living or dead – is produced for examination. However, if a suitable example, or type specimen to use the scientific term, were produced the beast would be accepted as a known animal.

And yet there is ample proof that some, at least, of these cryptids are real animals. The existence of the Sasquatch is supported by an impressive mass of evidence and the quality of some of it is very convincing. However, it must be admitted that the remaining evidence can be of poor quality; in some instances it has even been falsified by hoaxers. A smaller amount of evidence points to the existence of the other man-beast cryptids, but what there is can be extremely persuasive. Even so, most scientists refuse to accept the reality of these beasts.

The purpose of this book is to study and review the evidence for the existence of these cryptid man-like or ape-like creatures. But before launching into the hunt for the unknown, it is as well to deal with a few general points and principles.

First, it is important to be clear that a great many cryptids have been accepted as known animals by the scientific world. Among these have been the gorilla and the okapi, both of which were the subject of wild tales among the tribesmen of Africa.

These tales were widely discounted by European scientists and the creatures were written off as fabulous. But when a type specimen was produced, the scientific world rapidly accepted the reality of the beasts and set off to investigate them thoroughly.

Those days are not yet over – cryptids are still sneaking into reality. Around 20 new species of mammal alone have been accepted by science every year since the mid-1990s. Most of these beasts are fairly small and are simply new species of already accepted types of animal. But not all of them.

People living in the Vietnamese forests have for years been telling Europeans about a large antelope-like creature that is very rare, very shy and lives in the dense mountain forests of the Nghe An and Ha Tinh provinces. Nobody took the tales seriously until 1992, when a zoologist was handed a pair of horns that he could not identify. Such hard evidence demanded further investigation so an expedition was organized and sent into the mountains. Within a very short time the members of the party had been shown one of the mystery creatures by local huntsmen. The saola has been accepted as a known animal ever since. There are thought to be only a few hundred of them browsing on leaves in the forests but whether the animal is part of the bovine species or is a type of antelope or goat remains unclear.

The fact that such a large mammal could live unknown to science came as something of a surprise to many people. It indicates that it is possible for large animals to hide from science with surprising ease, given the right conditions.

Many people who are engaged in the hunt for cryptids – they are generally known as cryptozoologists – can feel resentment towards the scientific establishment as a whole and some individual scientists in particular. There is a feeling that scientists have deliberately closed their minds to the possible existence of cryptid hominoids. Any evidence put forward is dismissed as mistaken, or a hoax, sometimes after no more than a cursory examination. Some scientists seem determined to prove that such cryptids do not exist, to the extent that several have been accused of wilfully misinterpreting data to back up their stance.

In some instances such criticism is no doubt justified, but to be fair to scientists as a whole it must be acknowledged that they often work under constraints. The scientists working in areas most closely related to cryptid hominoids are zoologists studying primates. They might spend much of their time teaching students and marking papers and any time that they devote to research must be funded by universities or public bodies of one kind or another. Research funding is much in demand. It is generally only awarded to projects that are put forward by scientists who are already experienced in the field and so have a reasonable chance of producing a significant result. It also helps if the research project includes something that is currently fashionable in the academic world – a prime example being climate change in the years after 2005.

Sasquatch, Yetis and the like simply do not fit into this pattern. The study of these creatures is not supported by a mass of pre-existing data, it does not offer a good chance of a significant result and it is not promoted by scientists already highly experienced in the field of cryptid hominoids – because there aren't any. Above all, this field is not fashionable in the way that climate change is so the chances of any scientist getting research backing are practically nil. Some scientists who have chosen to devote some of their time to cryptids have been instructed by their employers to

drop the subject and spend their time studying something more likely to produce a positive result. Scientists are only human in that they often have families to support and so, understandably, do not want to fall foul of their employers.

That said a growing number of scientists are willing to devote much of their spare time to looking into cryptid hominoids. Because they are prepared to analyse evidence collected by field researchers, who are inevitably not professional scientists, they have produced a body of evidence that something is living out there. At the same time, they have also successfully identified hoaxes and misidentification.

It can be surprisingly easy to misidentify something, particularly if it is a living creature seen only fleetingly in poor light conditions. In July 1978 three 12-year-old

The vast forests of the Pacific Northwest region offer plenty of space in which an unrecognized species of ape could survive.

boys reported meeting a human-like animal near Ottosen in Iowa. They were walking back from school when they saw the creature standing upright in a cornfield. It was, they said, 5 feet (152 cm) tall. It had deep-set eyes and it was covered in brown fur. As the startled boys stood watching, the being watched them back. When they began to retreat, the beast dropped down on all fours and shook its head and then it moved off to investigate some trash bins. The boys fled, but looking back they saw the thing rummaging for food, sometimes on four feet and sometimes on two.

The creature was identified as a Bigfoot. However, its appearance, behaviour and way of moving sounds very much like that of a bear. It is much more likely that the creature was a bear and that the boys mistook what they saw.

In 1988 a strange animal was found dead on a highway in Florida. Those who saw it were convinced it was a cougar. This caused some excitement because the cougar has been extinct in Florida for generations although there have been reports of a distinct species of cougar in the Eastern United States. The body was studied, but it turned out to be that of a large tawny-coloured domestic dog that had become bloated as decomposition had set in with the Florida heat.

> In October 1985 the Pennsylvania police force arrested a man and charged him with wasting police time. He had been in the habit of dressing up in a gorilla suit...

There have also been hoaxes. In October 1985 the Pennsylvania police force arrested a man and charged him with wasting police time. He had been in the habit of dressing up in a gorilla suit and then going out at night to prance about alongside remote rural roads, scaring passers-by. Several passing motorists had reported a Bigfoot sighting to the local police after seeing the man. Of course, the police never found a Bigfoot but they wasted several hours looking for one. The man was fined $50.

Against this background of hoax and error it is perhaps understandable that many scientists look askance at the whole cryptid field. It would do their reputations and their employment prospects no good at all to become the victim of a hoax or to mistake a bear for an unknown species of ape.

The study and documentation of these cryptids is, therefore, largely left to non-professionals. Some pop out to the woods for a weekend here and there, others devote almost their entire lives to the quest. The amount of evidence they have produced is amazing and it forms the basis for this book. No tributes to these people and their dedication can be enough because they have spent huge amounts of time and money on the quest.

This quest is not only demanding in terms of time and money: it can also be dangerous. In October 1989 Bruce Davis and his wife went missing in Florida. Davis had spent years searching for the Skunk Ape, a Florida variant of the Sasquatch that we will be looking at later in this book. The police found the couple's car first and then their overturned canoe was discovered some 12 miles (19 km) away. Their bodies were never recovered so presumably some tragic accident overtook them.

There may also be some confusion over 'hominid' and 'hominoid', the terms that are used when discussing cryptid animals of the type dealt with in this book. In scientific terms a hominoid is an animal that belongs to the ape family. Gorillas and chimpanzees are both hominoids, as are numerous species of extinct apes known through fossils. Hominids are creatures that belong to the genus Homo, or are immediately ancestral to such animals. So far as has been definitely proven there is only one hominid living today: ourselves. Numerous extinct hominids are known from fossils but these remains are frequently only partial and there is much controversy about how the different fossil hominids are related to each other and to modern humans.

Finally, I should explain why the names of these cryptid beasts are capitalized. For instance, the Australian cryptid hominoid is the Yowie, not the yowie. The system was developed by Richard Greenwell in 1986 when he was editor of the *Journal of the International Society of Cryptozoology*. The problem was that some cryptids were known to locals and to cryptozoologists by a variety of names. To bring order to the confusion, Greenwell decided that any local or informal names for a cryptid should be given in italics, while the most widely used name for that animal among cryptozoologists should be in roman type, but take a capital letter. However, if the cryptid became accepted it should adopt its cryptozoological name in lower case roman type.

Thus the mysterious ape of the Himalayas might be referred to by scientists as the 'yeh-ti', the 'metoh kangmi' or the 'bad manshi'. Or it might be the Yeti. If the creature is ever proved to exist it would be known as the yeti. Such neat distinctions are for the scientist, however. Most writers simply write about the Sasquatch, the Yeti or the Yowie.

It is to be hoped that before long even scientists will be writing about the sasquatch, not the Sasquatch; the yeti, not the Yeti; the orang pendek, not the Orang Pendek; and perhaps even the yowie, not the Yowie.

1 Frontier Tales

First Impressions

The Sasquatch, or Bigfoot, hit the world's headlines in 1958 when the members of a construction crew building a road through the Bluff Creek area of remote northern California were thrown into panic when their worksite was visited by an elusive beast that threw their tools about and left footprints that looked human – except for their enormous size. The local newspaper dubbed the unseen creature 'Bigfoot'.

In 1851 two hunters in Greene County, Arkansas watched a Sasquatch apparently trying to catch a calf from a herd of domestic cattle.

One of the workmen, Jerry Crew, poured plaster of Paris into one of the footprints, thereby producing a solid piece of evidence. The photograph of that footprint cast, paired with the evocative name of Bigfoot, propelled the story out of the local media and on to the national, and then the international, stage.

But the Jerry Crew encounter of 1958 was very far from being the first time that the Sasquatch or Bigfoot had been come across by humans. While some investigators were concentrating on the footprints around Bluff Creek and elsewhere, others were looking back into the past. They reasoned that if the mystery footprint-maker was a real creature it must have been encountered before: it had.

The native peoples of North America are the source of the oldest stories about the Sasquatch. As might be expected, each tribe had its own name for this creature. The Iroquois called it the *wendigo* or the *wittiko*, the Micmac called it the *chenoo* and the Penobscott used the name *kiwakwe*.

European folklorists, the first people to come across these stories in any number, used the general term 'Wendigo'. However, they treated the tales as little better than fairy stories and concentrated on the fictional element, no matter how much the native peoples insisted that the creatures were real. The problem with these early reports, from a scientific point of view, is that they are not only rather vague but they also contain no details of time or place. They simply talk about the animals as they might talk about bear or elk. The creatures are described as being covered all over in fur and looking like a very large human. It is said that they avoid humans and live in remote forested areas, where they are active mostly at night.

Interestingly the further away from forested mountains that researchers got, the more the stories they collected about this creature became detached from reality. While the tribes of British Columbia treated the Sasquatch as just another animal, albeit a rather special one that was akin to humans, the Ojibway of the plains regarded it as a messenger from the gods. The appearance of a Sasquatch was seen as a bad omen, a sign that supernatural trouble was on the way.

The name Sasquatch comes from the writings of J.W. Burns, who was a teacher on the Chehalis Indian Reserve in British Columbia. It is an anglicization of the word that is more properly rendered as *sesqec*, but the name has now stuck. Although it was at first used more widely in Canada than the United States, many researchers now prefer it to the tabloid-sounding 'Bigfoot'. So far as Burns was concerned, though, he was just collecting folktales and legends with no basis in reality. Like others working with the indigenous peoples, he did not take the stories of gigantic hairy man-apes seriously.

But J.W. Burns soon realized that the tribesmen considered the Sasquatch to be all too real. In May 1938 he was at a local festival when an official from the Canadian government touched on the subject. 'Of course,' the speaker said, 'Sasquatch are merely imaginary Indian monsters. No white man has ever seen them and they do not exist.' The speaker then found himself pushed out of the way by Chief Flying Eagle of the Halkomelem. 'The white speaker is wrong,' declared Flying Eagle. 'Some white men have seen Sasquatch. Many Indians have seen them. Sasquatch are still all around here. I have spoken.'

Hairy ape-men

Chief Flying Eagle was right – white men had been reporting sightings of the hairy ape-man of the woods for some years. As far back as 1793 the *Boston Gazette* was reporting on a big, hairy and unidentified creature called the 'chickly cuddly', a term that seems to be an anglicization of a Cherokee word that translated as 'hairy man thing'. Details of what the creature looked like or what it did are, however, lacking.

The oldest known contemporary account of a Sasquatch sighting comes from the 22 September 1818 edition of the *Watchman* newspaper, in New York State. This report states that a few days earlier, near Ellisburgh, a 'gentleman of unquestionable veracity' saw 'an animal resembling the Wild Man of the Woods'. This would seem to indicate that the supposed 'Wild Man of the Woods' was already a well-known figure of legend or rumour. The creature was described as being like a large man, but covered in hair. It walked out of the trees and on to a road, a few yards from the witness. Seeing the human, the creature turned and ran off, leaning forwards as it did so. It left footprints behind it that were human-like but very wide at the toes.

In 1851 two hunters in Greene County, Arkansas watched a Sasquatch apparently in the act of trying to catch a calf from a herd of domestic cattle. They described the creature as being:

'... an animal bearing the unmistakable likeness of humanity. He was of gigantic stature, the body being covered with hair and the head with long locks that fairly enveloped the neck and shoulders.'

As soon as the creature realized that humans were in the vicinity it stopped chasing the cattle and instead stared at the hunters. It then turned and ran off at high speed, leaving behind human-like footprints that were 13 inches (32 cm) long. The newspaper that reported the incident speculated that the creature was a human survivor of an earthquake that had taken place in 1811. It was thought that he had taken to an animal-like existence in order to survive and so had acquired animal-like hair and an appearance to go with it. This was a common theory in the 19th century.

Mysterious intruder

In the 1860s, newspapers in Michigan reported that similar creatures had been seen several times around the Lake Saint Clair region. A little later, in 1869, 'wild men' were reported as having been seen in Iowa while the Pennsylvania newspapers carried similar stories in 1874, followed by Indiana newspaper reports in 1895 and 1897.

One of the most detailed and interesting of these mid-19th century reports came from a hunter working near Antioch, California, in 1869. He had found a good site on which to pitch his camp but soon noticed that while he was out hunting during the day something had come into the area. The ashes of his fire had been scattered around and there were footprints that looked like those of a man, except for their immense size. Curious, the man decided to hide in a patch of brush which gave him a good view of his camp. After two hours he was rewarded when the mysterious intruder arrived.

'The creature, whatever it was, stood 5 feet [152 cm] high and disproportionately broad and square at the shoulders, with arms of great length. The legs were very short and the body long. The head was small compared with the rest of the creature and appeared to be set upon his shoulders without a neck. The whole was covered with dark brown and cinnamon-coloured hair, quite long on some parts, on the head standing in a shock and growing close down to the eyes.'

After looking around carefully, the creature kicked the embers of the camp fire and then it bent down and picked up a stick which it whirled around its head, producing a circle of smoke. After the glowing end of the stick had gone out, the beast threw its head back and whistled, after which it picked up a second stick and again swung it around. After about 15 minutes the creature 'was joined by another – a female unmistakably – when both turned and walked past me, within 20 yards of where I sat, and disappeared into the brush.' Given the date of the encounter, the writer's reference to the second creature being unmistakably female would probably mean that it had breasts.

The hunter concluded by saying that he had met one other hunter who had seen the creatures and about a dozen more who had seen mysterious gigantic human-like footprints. This acceptance of the reality of the creatures by those who spent a lot of time in the forested hills is a feature of these early cases that surfaces again and again. The educated townsfolk who wrote and read the newspapers were amazed by the stories of wild men but the hunters and trappers were not.

In 1895 a man by the name of Riley Smith was picking berries near Winsted, Connecticut, when his bulldog came dashing out of a patch of woodland. It was whimpering and trying to hide behind him. Smith stood up to see 'a large man, stark naked and covered with hair all over his body' emerge from the trees. The instant the 'wild man' saw Smith it gave a terrifying yell, then turned and fled back into the woods. Smith later admitted that he had been paralyzed with fear.

Meanwhile, these unusual creatures were beginning to be called 'gorillas' in newspaper reports, in deference to the newly discovered great apes of the African forests. The idea that the sightings were of men gone wild was gradually dropped in favour of the idea that they were gorillas or similar apes escaped from zoos or travelling shows. As a newspaper reported from Arkansas:

> 'If this meets the eye of any showman who has lost one of his collection of beasts, he may know where to find it. At present it is the terror of all women and children in the valley. It cannot be caught and nobody is willing to shoot it.'

This last comment is interesting because it is the first appearance in print of a feature of many later Sasquatch sightings. Several hunters have had a Sasquatch square in the sights of their rifle, only to find themselves unwilling to shoot. There is something about the Sasquatch that seems to be so human that it would make killing one

Smith stood up to see 'a large man, stark naked and covered with hair all over his body' emerge from the trees. The instant the 'wild man' saw Smith it gave a terrifying yell, then turned and fled back into the woods. Smith later admitted that he had been paralyzed with fear.

something like murder. Others have been less squeamish and have blasted away at a Sasquatch without compunction but, at least to date, without much effect.

Unruly visitor

In 1904 an Oregon newspaper reported an attack on a miner's log cabin by a 'gorilla'. William Ward and his friend Burlison were sitting by the stove in their cabin when they heard something big and heavy walking around outside. The thing sounded as if it was walking on two feet like a man, not on all fours. After some minutes, the thing grabbed hold of one corner of the cabin and gave it a vigorous shake. Ward ran to the door with his rifle, but by then the beast was walking off into the darkness. He shot once, but missed. A few nights later the creature was back, and this time it tried to break down the door. Again Ward opened the door as the creature was moving off and again he opened fire. This time a rock weighing over four pounds came hurtling out of the darkness, but it missed him just as he had missed the creature.

The newspaper report subsequently concluded: 'Many of the miners in the district avow that the "wild man" is a reality. They have seen him and know whereof they speak. They say he is something after the fashion of a gorilla and unlike anything else that has ever been known; and not only that but he can throw rocks with wonderful force and accuracy. He is about 7 feet high [213 cm], has broad hands and feet and his body is covered by a prolific growth of hair. In short, he looks like the very devil.'

> 'Many of the miners in the district avow that the "wild man" is a reality. He is about 7 feet high… and his body is covered by hair. In short, he looks like the very devil.'

The Battle of Ape Canyon

Then in 1924 the *Oregonian* newspaper from Portland carried a story that was unlike the others. The report began by mentioning the 'mountain gorillas' that had been leaving gigantic footprints around the Mount St Helens area for some years and noted that 'Indians have been told of the mountain devils for sixty years'. It then detailed the occasions on which five gold prospectors had been attacked by these 'gorillas' panning for gold around the Lewis River, close to Mount St Helens. Amazingly, one of those prospectors, Fred Beck, was still alive when the Bigfoot stories of 1958 hit the headlines. When he was tracked down and interviewed he supplied extra details that were not included in the 1924 newspaper report.

The barren high mountains are where folklore and myth usually locate beasts of supernatural origin,
but the Sasquatch is firmly placed in more temperate forests and thus more likely to genuinely exist.

Beck and his colleagues – Marion Smith, Roy Smith, Gabe Lafever and John Peterson – had been working their claim for over two years by the time of the encounter. They had come across several footprints about 14 inches (35 cm) long in that time but after the initial excitement that they had caused the men ignored them. Then, in July 1924, they began to hear a noise as if somebody was banging loudly on a hollow wooden trunk. After that they heard a loud whistling call come from a wooded ridge that overlooked their camp. After a week of this, the men habitually carried their rifles with them when collecting firewood or water.

One day Marion Smith and Beck were fetching water when they saw one of the 'mountain gorillas'; it was about 100 yards away. It stood about 7 feet (213 cm) tall on its hind legs and it was watching the two men from behind a pine tree. Smith fired three shots but only hit the tree, so the creature ran off uninjured. When it reappeared from the trees, now about 200 yards away, Beck fired but he missed. They ran back to the cabin to consult with the others. Faced by gigantic man-like creatures, the prospectors decided to flee. However, it was getting late in the day, so they decided to stay the night rather than risk being caught in the woods in the dark with the 'mountain gorillas'.

Midnight attack

At midnight the men were rudely awoken by a terrific thump as something hit the cabin wall. The sound of heavy footfalls came from outside the cabin and Smith peered out through a chink between the logs to see three of the huge creatures. It also sounded as if there were others nearby. The creatures then picked up large rocks with which they began to pound at the walls, which prompted the men to grab their guns and prepare to face the beasts if they should break in.

At least two of the apes got on to the roof and began jumping up and down. Another began pounding on the door, which Beck braced shut with a wooden pole. After several terrifying minutes the assault ended and the creatures slipped away into the darkness, but less than an hour later they were back. Again they attacked the cabin, trying to break in, and again they retreated, only to return with redoubled fury to the assault. Finally, as dawn broke, the creatures left.

When the beings did not return for some time, the terrified miners gingerly opened the door and peered outside. All was quiet. They packed up and set off with as much as they could carry, leaving behind over $200 worth of equipment – no small loss in the days when the dollar was worth far more than it is today. As they set off down the trail towards civilization, the men saw one of the creatures emerge from the trees just 80 yards away. Beck whipped out his rifle and fired and this time he did not miss. The creature folded up and then collapsed. Falling over the edge of a canyon it dropped 400 feet (122 m) to the rocks below.

It was the last that the men saw of the creatures. When they got to Spirit Lake they reported their experience to the local rangers. The story soon got out and a team of armed reporters hurried up into the hills to find the cabin. Although some days had passed, the signs of the assault were still to be seen and the cabin was surrounded by gigantic footprints – some of which were ominously fresh. The reporters, like the miners, got out quickly.

> The signs of the assault were still to be seen and the cabin was surrounded by gigantic footprints – some of which were ominously fresh.

The place where this amazing confrontation took place was dubbed Ape Canyon by the press and it is still known by that name to this day. In his old age Beck speculated that the monsters that he had encountered were some sort of guardian spirits of the wilderness region rather than being flesh and blood creatures. He said that they had come from another dimension and were supernatural beings. None of this was evident in the original 1924 report.

Ostman's Encounter

Soon after the newspapers carried the story of the Battle of Ape Canyon, rumours spread through the area that 'a young Swede' had been kidnapped by the 'mountain gorillas' and that he had lived with them for some time. The 'young Swede' turned out to be a Canadian of Swedish extraction named Albert Ostman. While he was happy to tell close friends about his bizarre experience, he remained tight-lipped in public and shunned all publicity. It was not until the Bigfoot reports of 1958 made the subject rather more respectable that Ostman decided to go public. He had, he said, been afraid of public ridicule until then.

Even so, Ostman has never been one to court publicity. He has told his story to the newspapers a couple of times, and to Sasquatch investigators, but he has not otherwise sought either money or fame. The story began in the summer of 1924 when Ostman was working on a construction site in British Columbia. He decided to take a break and went up into the mountains inland of Toba Inlet in order to look for one of the many small

Albert Ostman claimed to have been taken by a family of Bigfoot apes and held prisoner for several days.

gold deposits that exist in that region. He camped out with just a sleeping bag, rather than a tent, because the weather was warm. Then when he returned to camp one night he noticed that his things had been disturbed as if somebody had been rummaging through them. Blaming animals looking for food, Ostman decided to tuck his rifle into his sleeping bag so that it would be handy in case a bear appeared. He promised himself that he would secure the food before leaving camp next day but he never got the chance.

At some point he was woken up by being pushed roughly down into his sleeping bag, which was then picked up and thrown over something. Ostman's first thought was that he had been thrown over a horse by bandits of some kind. Then he realized that the movement of the thing carrying him was not like that of a horse, but more like a man's. He felt a second bag filled with cans and equipment bumping against him and deduced that his captor had also grabbed his sealed bag of supplies.

After a while, Ostman felt that they were going up a steep hill. Then they began to go downhill, at which point the sleeping bag was dumped on the ground and dragged along for a while. It was again picked up and carried but after about three hours of this it was dropped on to the ground for the last time. It rolled downhill for a short distance and then stopped and Ostman could hear what sounded like chattering and grunting.

Captured by ape-men

Cautiously he poked his head out of the sleeping bag. At first he could see little, because it was dark, but as the dawn came up he could gradually distinguish four huge figures. They proved to be massively muscled, hairy ape-like men. There was a large male, who was clearly the leader, an equally large female and two smaller figures, one male and one female. Ostman guessed that he was seeing the mountain ape men that the local Indians had told him about and that he had been captured by a family group.

Recovering from his shock, Ostman reasoned that the creature who had brought him here must have had plenty of opportunity to kill him if it had wanted to do so. Looking around, he saw that they were in a small area of about seven acres, which was surrounded by sheer rocks which had only one visible opening. The older male sat there as if keeping watch. Realizing that he was being left alone, Ostman set out to explore the area. He found a source of water, emptied his sack of stores and set up camp, all the time watching for a way out.

The younger creatures had at first seemed frightened of him, but by the end of the first day they seemed more accepting. Ostman rolled an empty snuff box towards the young male, who picked up the shiny object with interest. When he found out how to open and close the box, the young male delightedly took it to the young female and showed her. Then he went to the older male and sat chattering to him for some time. Apart from being offered some roots and leaves to eat, Ostman was ignored but when he tried to leave, the older male blocked his way and glared at him. He considered shooting his way out but he had only six bullets and did not think that this would be enough to kill four such massive animals.

For several days Ostman camped out with his kidnappers, which gave him plenty of time to study them and their behaviour. The two larger creatures were over 7 feet (213 cm) tall, the younger ones around 6 feet (183 cm). All of them were massively built, with huge barrel chests of up to 55 (137 cm) inches and waists of 40 inches (101 cm). Ostman guessed their weight at over 600 lb. Their heads were flat-faced like those of humans but were small in relation to their bodies and they met the body without a noticeable neck. They had low foreheads which sloped up to a peak at the rear, although some of this was made up of stiff hair rather than bone and muscle. Their teeth were big and strong and although the older male had enlarged incisors they were not big enough to be called tusks. Heavily muscled arms, longer in proportion than a human's, ended in hands that were very large, with short and stubby fingers that had fingernails like chisels. Their feet were massive in size and the soles were heavily padded, like the pads on a dog's feet, but otherwise they were like those of a human. The younger female had smaller breasts than the older female so Ostman guessed that she and the younger male were juveniles that had not yet fully matured.

> **Their heads were flat-faced like those of humans but were small in relation to their bodies and they met the body without a noticeable neck.**

The creatures were active both by day and by night. They slept on what Ostman called blankets – sheets of woven bark and moss. Each day one or two of the creatures left to search for food, bringing back grass, roots and leaves. Ostman did not see them eat meat of any kind. When they were not out looking for food the two older creatures rested. The younger ones, by contrast, would play games and lark about. The male had a game in which he would hold his feet in his hands and then bounce along on his backside as if seeing how far he could get without touching the ground with any of his limbs. When they sat down or stood up, they came down from the upright to squatting in a single movement without using their arms to support themselves at all.

After several days of this, Ostman got a small fire going and brewed himself up some coffee. The smell attracted the two males, who came and sat down about 10 feet (305 cm) from him. Ostman poured himself some coffee and spread butter on some biscuits and the two creatures watched him carefully as he ate and drank. When he had finished his meal, Ostman opened a new snuff box and took a pinch. The older male then reached forward, took the box and emptied the entire contents into his mouth.

A few seconds later he began to squeal and claw at his tongue. He rolled over, then leapt up and dashed for the spring of water. The other creatures went after him as if they were worried. Ostman realized two things instantly. Firstly, the exit from the little valley was unguarded for the first time since he had arrived and secondly the old male might prove to be angry with him. Ostman grabbed his rifle and his bag of supplies and then ran for the exit. He was almost there when he heard footsteps behind him. He looked over his shoulder to see the older female running towards him. Dropping his bag, Ostman turned and fired a shot over her head. The female stopped instantly and bolted in the other direction. Grabbing his bag again, Ostman ran out of the valley and continued for over a mile before he paused.

He then scrambled up a slope so that he could look back towards his captors. There was no sign of pursuit, but even so he decided to take no chances. He walked all day, stopping only to shoot and cook a grouse before moving on. Two days later he stumbled across a small group of lumberjacks who took him in and gave him a meal before driving him down to their base camp. From there Ostman was able to make his way to Vancouver. He never went prospecting in the mountains again.

Muchalat Harry

At 3.00 am one autumn morning in 1928 a fur trapper from the Nootka tribe called Muchalat Harry came paddling back to his home on Vancouver Island in his canoe. Dressed only in his underwear and suffering from exposure he was clearly terrified. Because he was babbling the family sent for the local missionary, Father Anthony. It was Father Anthony who recorded the story and so preserved it for later generations.

Muchalat left his home and headed for the Conuma River, at the head of Tlupana Inlet, where he intended to spend several weeks trapping fur. He paddled some way upriver, then cached his canoe and walked 12 miles (19 km) inland to what he thought was a promising fur area. After pitching camp he set his trap line and settled down to business. All seemed set for a routine trip.

One night he was jerked awake by being roughly picked up. Wrapped in his blankets

After the Bigfoot encounter, the Chapmans abandoned their wooden cabin which fell into disrepair.

but otherwise clad only in underwear he was thrown over the shoulder of a big hairy man-like creature. Muchalat had heard stories about the Sasquatch since his childhood, so unlike Ostman he immediately guessed what was happening. He struggled, but the creature held him firmly. Muchalat estimated that he had been carried for about three miles before being dumped on the ground beside a steep hill with a rock overhang.

Collecting himself, he looked about and was alarmed to see himself surrounded by about 20 Sasquatch. The bigger males were pushing the females and the young back from him, as if to keep them safe. His alarm turned to terror when he saw a pile of bones lying on the ground because they showed obvious signs of having been gnawed. Muchalat was convinced that he had been brought in as prey and would soon be killed and eaten. He backed nervously against the rock while first one, then another male Sasquatch came up to him.

The Sasquatch seemed fascinated by his underwear, which they plucked at repeatedly. Muchalat guessed that they thought it was some kind of loose second skin. After a while the males lost interest and allowed the females and the young to get closer to the terrified Muchalat. When it was fully light the majority of the adults left, presumably to search for food, and Muchalat was left with the young and a couple of adult females. An hour or so after noon the two females lay down to rest, so he fled.

He ran downhill, hoping to find a river, which he did. After running downstream for about 15 miles, as fast as his legs could carry him, he found his canoe and then leapt in and started paddling. There was no sign of pursuit, but Muchalat did not care. He just wanted to get home.

Muchalat Harry was confined to bed by Father Anthony and it was three weeks before the missionary would let him leave his home. It was during this time that Muchalat Harry told Father Anthony about his experiences. It was decided that Muchalat should keep quiet about the bizarre events, although he discussed it with his friends and Father Anthony wrote it all down. Muchalat Harry never went back to the Conuma River to collect his rifle, equipment and furs. Nor did he ever go alone into the forests again.

The Ruby Creek Incident

Another early incident that was recorded at the time, but which remained largely unknown until after 1958, was the so-called Ruby Creek Incident. Again, the witnesses chose to remain silent in public for fear of ridicule. It was only when Bigfoot became widely known that the witnesses were willing to be quoted in the press. The incident took place in the summer of 1941 just outside the settlement of Ruby Creek near Agassiz in British Columbia and it involved the Chapmans, a local family living in a small shack. Mrs Jennie Chapman and her three children tended crops of vegetables and fruit around the house while George Chapman worked on the railways. He was often away for several days on end so he was absent during the episode.

It was about three in the afternoon when the oldest boy, aged nine, came back to the house saying that he had seen a cow-like animal coming down the forested hill near the cabin. He seemed rather worried, so Mrs Chapman went to investigate. She saw the head and shoulders of what she took to be a bear moving through the undergrowth, though it seemed to be very large and it was behaving oddly. She called the two other children – aged seven and five – who came trotting in from the fields.

Then the creature stepped out of the underbrush and Mrs Chapman saw at once that it was no bear. In fact, it looked like a gigantic man, covered all over in dense hair of a brownish-ochre colour. Judging by a fencepost that it was standing close to, the creature was about 7 feet 6 inches (228 cm) tall.

Its shoulders were broad and its chest was massive although its head was small in comparison with its huge body and there did not seem to be a neck. The creature's arms were longer than those of a human, reaching almost to the knees. Its face and the palms of its hands were bare of hair and coloured very dark brown or almost black.

The creature looked about and then seemed to see Mrs Chapman and her eldest son. It threw its head back and emitted a cry that sounded like a gurgle that became a loud whistle. After that it began striding purposefully across the field towards the house. It showed no fear of humans and no hesitation about approaching a house.

Now seriously alarmed, Mrs Chapman sent her eldest boy into the house to grab a blanket. She then held the blanket out in front of her and shepherded the two younger children under it so that the creature would not be able to see them. She later said that she had done this because she thought the creature had seen the younger children go into the house. If it did not see them leave it might go into the house to look for them rather than follow the family downstream, thus giving Mrs Chapman and her children a vital few minutes head start. She then led her three children away from the house and down the steep slope to the Ruby Creek. Once they were out of sight of the creature the four took to their heels and fled downstream towards the village. Once there, they made for Mrs Chapman's father's house where they poured out their story, after which they were given food and allowed to rest.

A still from a video that claims to show a Bigfoot moving through the forest, though the detail is a little blurred.

Two hours later George Chapman came home from work. The first thing he saw was the front door standing wide open and the door to the outhouse smashed in as if by some terrific force. In some loose soil nearby he saw the unmistakeable giant footprints of a 'wild man of the woods'. Now alarmed he called out for his family, but after getting no response he searched the house. He could find no sign of them but then he then saw the tracks of his wife and three children heading off for the creek. There was no sign of the giant footprints following them, so George relaxed slightly. He followed his family's tracks until he was certain that they had not been followed, then returned to the house.

The smashed door to the outhouse was a robust affair designed to frustrate bears, so George was amazed that anything could have destroyed it with such apparent ease. Inside he found the family's store of food scattered about and half-eaten. In particular a

55-gallon barrel of salt fish had been smashed open and the contents thrown everywhere. He then set off to track down the intruder. It had walked over a potato field down to the creek and then returned to the hill before going back into the forest from which it had emerged. Chapman guessed it had gone an hour or so before he arrived.

He then headed for his father-in-law's house where he found his shaken family. They returned to the house with Chapman's father-in-law and a brace of rifles. Next day, Chapman's father-in-law stayed at the house with his rifle while Chapman went to work. There was no sign of the Sasquatch that day, but the following evening the family heard the strange call again and found footprints near their house. It came back for five more nights, then was heard of no more.

The Sightings Continue

Meanwhile the less spectacular sightings continued unabated. In 1936 a couple from the Aleut tribe came back from working the farm to their home near Lake Iliamna in Alaska to find their 8-year-old daughter in a state of some alarm. The girl was accustomed to being left at home, and knew all about bears and other local wildlife. She said that while she had been playing on the kitchen floor she had heard movement outside. Peering out she had seen three very tall, hairy men walking around the barn. The creatures walked upright, just like humans and were covered in reddish-brown hair. Two of them headed for the garbage dump and began rooting about as if looking for food, while the third headed for the open door of the cabin. The creatures, the girl said, seemed to be communicating by using soft whistling noises.

Cowering back as the creature approached, the girl began to be scared. The giant figure reached the doorway, put its hand on the door lintel and bent down to peer inside. The door was about 5 and a half feet (167 cm) tall, so the girl later estimated that the beast must have been about 7 feet (213 cm) tall. As the creature looked in a powerful stink invaded the room, an offensive smell like animal musk. Then a loud whistling call came from outside, at which the creature stepped back from the door, stood upright and looked around. It then whistled in answer before turning and walking off. A few minutes later the girl's parents arrived. Presumably it had been their approach that had caused the creatures to leave.

In 1937 Jane Patterson set off to pick rhubarb in the run-wild garden of an abandoned shack near her home at Bridesville in British Columbia. She walked into the garden and around a bush to find a large hairy animal sitting on the ground about 15 feet (4.5 m) away. It was busily engaged in picking rhubarb. The creature stood up, revealing itself to be a hair-covered human-like creature of massive bulk that stood about 6 feet (183 cm) tall. 'Oh, hello,' said Miss Patterson in surprise. The creature blinked at her. She backed off slowly and quietly while the creature watched her, then as soon as she was out of sight she fled.

In 1939 a prospector named Burns Yeomans was near Harrison Lake, British Columbia, when he saw a group of five creatures in a clearing about a thousand yards away. He described the beasts as being big and hairy like bears but shaped more like massive humans. Two of the creatures were wrestling with each other, while the others watched. Intrigued, Yeomans also sat down to watch. The wrestling continued for almost half an hour until one of the wrestlers appeared to give up, at which point the creatures walked off into the woods.

Two years later, Clayton Mack of the Bella Coola tribe of British Columbia was in a boat heading up the coast toward Quatna to do some fishing. He saw what he thought was a bear standing on its hind legs on the beach. There was something a bit odd about the 'bear', so Mack turned his boat towards it. When he was about 400 yards offshore, the creature turned to look at him.

It was then that Mack realized that whatever the creature was, it was no bear, so he studied it more closely. It was about 8 feet (244 cm) tall and it had broad shoulders and a smallish head with no obvious neck. The creature then turned and strode off on two legs toward the trees that came down close to the water's edge. As it reached the treeline, the creature turned again, twisting its head round to gaze briefly at Mack. Then it entered the trees and vanished from sight.

William Roe's Account

The sighting by William Roe in 1955 remains a classic for many reasons. Not only was Roe an unimpeachable witness who was widely known to be trustworthy and reliable, but his report included a wealth of detail that is rarely found. Most people who encounter a Sasquatch are so surprised by the sudden confrontation that they fail to note details – not so Roe.

At the time of his encounter with a Sasquatch, Roe was a middle-aged man living in Alberta, Canada. He had been born in the backwoods of Michigan and had been familiar with North American wildlife from birth. After he married he spent some years in

Canada working as a trapper and hunter and it was this that brought him to the area around Tête Jaune Cache, Alberta, in October 1955.

About a year earlier he had shot a magnificent black bear on nearby Mica Mountain, but this particular trip was more by way of a reconnaissance. He carried his hunting rifle with him, but he was not really looking for a kill. Roe was alone and on foot as he approached an old abandoned mine that he knew about. By his own account, he had decided to have a poke around the workings just to pass the time of day. It was about 3.00 pm.

He was just stepping out into the clearing when he saw what he took to be a grizzly bear amongst the bushes on the far side. With the practised ease of a hunter, Roe silently stepped back into cover and squatted down to watch. At first he could see only the top of the creature's head, then a furry shoulder as it moved about in the bushes. When the creature emerged into the clearing and stood up it was immediately obvious that it was not a bear.

> As the creature looked back at him he saw a spark of humanity in its eyes.

Roe at first took it to be a huge man in a fur coat and then he thought that perhaps it was an actor dressed up as a gorilla for a movie – though he had not heard of any movie company at work in the area.

But as the creature ambled gently across the clearing towards him, Roe dismissed this idea, because it was bigger than any man he had ever seen and it moved in a peculiar way. The creature got to within 20 feet (6 m) of Roe before it stopped. It then squatted down on its haunches and began to eat leaves off a bush.

After a minute or two, the beast seemed to suddenly catch Roe's scent. It looked around, then fixed its eyes on his before shuffling back four steps and then standing up. It walked off rapidly, glancing back over its shoulder at the bush where Roe sat hidden. He raised his rifle to shoot what he now realized would be a very valuable specimen, but as the creature looked back at him he saw a spark of humanity in its eyes. He suddenly felt that killing this creature would be more like murder, so he let it go.

The creature stopped on the far side of the clearing. It tipped its head back, let rip with a call that was half-laugh and half-howl and then vanished into the woods. Roe saw it a few minutes later as it crossed a ridge about 200 yards distant. The creature again emitted its odd call and then was gone for good.

According to Roe's written account, the Sasquatch had stood well over 6 feet (183 cm) tall and had shoulders about 3 feet (91 cm) across. He guessed its weight at around 400 pounds and took it to be a female because it had a pair of large breasts and no obvious external penis. Its body fell straight from the shoulders to the hips, not curving in and out again as does that of a human, and it was covered with a dark brown fur about an inch or so long. The arms were heavily muscled and long in proportion, reaching almost to the knees and the feet were large, about five inches across. They had a grey-brown skin on their undersides. The creature put its heel down first when it walked, but it seemed to glide along without the up-and-down bobbing of a human stride.

The creature's head was higher at the back than at the front and its nose was broad and flat while the lips and chin jutted forward. Its ears were the same shape as those of a human, but its eyes were small and black – more like those of a bear. The skin around the eyes and mouth was bare of hair and the face was capable of expression. When it saw Roe the creature looked so amazed that Roe could not help grinning.

All these physical features have been reported time and again by those who claim to have seen the Sasquatch.

The Lull Before the Storm

In the autumn of 1957 the forests near Bend, Oregon were the scene of one of the very last sightings before the Bigfoot story hit the media. Gary Joanis and Jim Newall were out hunting when Joanis shot a deer in a clearing. He called Newall over and the two men began walking forward to pick up the deer. But they were beaten to it by a hairy creature that was walking on its hind legs like a human. The creature strode out of the trees, picked up the deer carcass then turned and started walking back. Annoyed that something was taking his kill, Joanis shouted. When the creature did not react, Joanis fired a shot. He was certain that he had hit the target, but apart from issuing a shrill whistle the departing giant showed no signs of having been injured. It strode into the woods with its stolen load and was swallowed up by the undergrowth.

The events of 1958 would change everything in the world of the Sasquatch, so it is worth pausing to reflect on the situation as it stood before the national and the international media got hold of the story. The pre-1958 reports are important for many reasons. Not the least of these is that they were made at a time when the vast majority of people had never heard of any supposed man-like ape living in North America. All of these reports were made in isolation from each other, separated by several years of time and hundreds of miles in distance. There is nothing to suggest that the men making the reports knew anything about the other stories. Indeed, most of them remained buried in archives and totally forgotten until after the 1958 events at Bluff Creek, when researchers began scouring old newspaper reports for accounts such as these.

And yet the reports are not only consistent with each other, but also with more recent sightings. The creatures that are seen are always described in a similar way, both in terms of appearance and behaviour. This alone would indicate that the reports are describing real creatures, even if they are rarely encountered.

The distribution of the reports is also interesting. They are made on the fringes of the settled areas, along the frontier of civilization. The earliest reports came from the Eastern States, but they tailed off as human population densities increased. Instead the focus shifts west to the areas where human populations remain low. Again, this indicates that a real animal is involved. Other large creatures such as cougar or bear were similarly encountered in eastern areas early in the 19th century, but are found there no longer. Looking at these pre-1958 reports, the American upright ape would seem to have abandoned its eastern range in the face of human pressure.

Nomadic beast

Again, encounters with these animals seem to have displayed a frequently repeated pattern. One or more of these creatures would be seen, or its footprints found, and it would then seem to hang around in the area for a few days before moving on. Again, behaviour such as this is typical of a nomadic animal with a large home territory. Ostman said that he had the impression that the camp at which he was held prisoner was just a temporary stopover. Why he thought this is not clear, but it fits in with the other evidence.

But although the creature was unknown to science, and unheard of in built-up areas, it was known about and accepted in more remote regions. Miners, trappers and indigenous peoples were well aware of the 'wild man' or 'mountain gorilla'. They knew it existed and that it was rarely encountered. Such knowledge was kept within a fairly tight circle of locals.

In 1958 that circle was about to be broken with dramatic results.

2 Big Foot Arrives

Incidents at Bluff Creek

The events of 1958 unfolded themselves with ever-increasing speed before an astonished and bewildered public that found itself torn between excitement and scepticism. Perhaps the stories got such wide coverage because reports about the Yeti had been filling the international news media for some years. Cryptozoology – though the word had not yet really caught on – was an acceptable news topic. Another reason was the availability of dramatic photographic evidence. Any reporter will confirm the fact that a good photograph will 'give legs' to a story and ensure that it continues to run, while the same story without a picture would soon die down and lose public interest.

The trail of events actually began in 1957 when work began on building a road through the Bluff Creek area of northern California. It was designed to aid the logging industry by opening the region up to heavy machinery. Ray Wallace was the head of the firm hired to do the job. His brother Wilbur was one of the team foremen in charge of the task of clearing a flat roadbed through the rugged and densely forested terrain. The Wallace company was an established construction outfit in the area and was running more than one project.

It was only after the event that workmen at a Wallace site near Mad River remembered that they had found some strange tracks in March 1958. Nobody could recall exactly what they looked like: at least one man said they were bear tracks, while another said they were faked by some unidentified prankster who wanted to spook the workmen. At this distance in time it is impossible to state anything definitive about this event, except that it was odd but quickly dismissed at the time. It is only later events that have given it any importance.

On 3 August the workmen on the Bluff Creek Road turned up for work to find some of their equipment disturbed. A spare tyre weighing around 700 lb had been rolled about, causing the men to wonder who or what had been interfering. On 27 August the workmen discovered that the site had again been visited by something odd overnight, but this time it had left footprints.

It was Gerald Crew, known as Jerry, who found them. They were impressed into the soft soil around his bulldozer. The footprints were later described as being exactly like those of a naked human foot, but much larger.

At first Crew thought that they must be some sort of practical joke, but after following the tracks about and studying them more closely he became convinced that they had really been left by a huge man of some kind. He went to see his foreman, Wilbur

You have to be quite brave to camp overnight at Bluff Creek, an area where some of the earliest Bigfoot encounters to hit the headlines took place.

Wallace, who came to look at the tracks. After some discussion it was decided to ignore the strange nocturnal intruder – as long as he did not turn up in daylight hours when the work crew were on site.

On 21 September the local newspaper, the *Humboldt Times*, printed a letter from Mrs Jesse Bemis about the events up at Bluff Creek. Jesse Bemis was the wife of one of the workmen on the site. The letter prompted the editor, Andrew Genzoli, to dig out some old stories along similar lines. Reporter Betty Allen then made the link between the mysterious giant footprints and the stories that had been circulating for years about a hairy man-ape that the white settlers and farmers called 'Big Foot'. Allen went out to talk to people who had actually seen the tracks of the man-ape. On 28 September she had a piece published about the creature she called 'Bigfoot', which summarized the evidence to date. She also suggested that next time somebody found any footprints they should take a cast using plaster of Paris.

Solid evidence

Then, on 1 October, Jerry Crew and the work gang at Bluff Creek found more footprints that had been left overnight around their worksite. Two of the workers promptly quit. Wilbur Wallace asked his brother and boss, Ray Wallace, to come up to Bluff Creek to go over the situation.

Meanwhile Jerry Crew called an old friend of his, Bob Titmus, who went to see Betty Allen to get some plaster of Paris and instructions on how to use it. On 3 October Titmus arrived at the worksite and, together with Crew, poured the plaster into the clearest of the footprints.

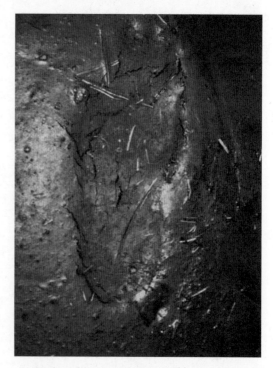

The cast was taken down to the offices of the *Humboldt Times* by Crew. The man and the cast were photographed and the amazing photograph was used to illustrate an article by Andrew Genzoli. It was the combination of a stunning photo, solid evidence and well-researched writing that propelled 'Bigfoot' into the national media. The story was taken up and reprinted across the USA and Canada and then filtered out to media in other countries.

Back at Bluff Creek, the excitement mounted

A Bigfoot footprint left in soft mud: the sheer size of the prints encountered by forest workers caused much excitement.

when on 12 October two workers – Ray Kerr and Bob Breazle – actually sighted the mysterious footprint-maker. Driving along a local dirt road after dark, they momentarily caught a gigantic upright figure in their headlights. The creature ran off into the woods, but the two men described a hairy human figure well over 6 feet (183 cm) tall. Within 48 hours another 13 men had left their jobs on the road construction project.

Meanwhile, Bob Titmus was out in the forests looking for signs of the mysterious creature. So far as is known he was the first man ever to go looking for Sasquatch. He found some more footprints and took casts.

In the meantime the events around Bluff Creek, followed by the newspaper reports, had attracted two Yeti investigators, John Green and René Dahinden. These two men were in touch with a Texas millionaire named Tom Slick whose interest in mystery animals and other odd phenomena made him willing to invest money in research. Also on the scene fairly quickly was the zoologist Ivan T. Sanderson who was writing a book about North American ecology at the time.

> Two workers actually sighted the mysterious footprint-maker. Driving along a local dirt road after dark, they caught a gigantic upright figure in their headlights.

With hindsight it is clear that the 1958 events on the Bluff Creek road construction site were crucial to the development of the Bigfoot enigma. First of all, the news story alerted the outside world to the existence of a large, hairy, man-like creature living in the forested hills and mountains of the Pacific northwest area – something the locals had known for years. But secondly it also galvanized a key group of men who would in varying ways have a dramatic impact on future research into what was then called Bigfoot.

Titmus, Green and Dahinden would all devote huge amounts of time, effort and money to the search for the mystery creature. Between them they amassed a vast number of footprint casts, eyewitness accounts, hair samples and other evidence. Sanderson would become the first, and for many years the only, serious scientist to recognize that there might be something in the reports. Slick would continue to provide the funds that made the work of the previous four possible. Ray Wallace would play an enigmatic and highly controversial role as the self-confessed perpetrator of all sorts of wild claims and hoaxes related to Bigfoot. Others, such as Crew and Allen, would drop out of the story fairly quickly.

Of all these men the most controversial proved to be Ray Wallace. For a start, he is known to have possessed a pair of gigantic wooden feet with which he went about faking Bigfoot tracks. Then he claimed that he had photographed and filmed Bigfoot on

A photographer lays a ruler down beside one of the Bluff Creek footprints before photographing it. The media exposure given to the footprints encouraged others to come forward to talk about earlier sightings.

several occasions. At another time he said that he had killed one of the creatures and had hidden its body away, though he never actually produced it.

A repeated claim was that Bigfoot lived in caves high in the mountains where they stored vast caches of gold nuggets. Wallace said that his motive for planting fake tracks was the desire to protect these gold stores. He was, most people agreed, a prankster with a unique sense of humour.

After his death in 2002 one of his relatives went so far as to claim that Wallace had 'invented Bigfoot' and that he had been responsible for nearly all the evidence that supported the idea that a giant man-ape existed in the Pacific Northwest. 'The reality is that Bigfoot just died', the newspapers announced after Wallace's death.

Practical joker

The big question that has never been properly answered to anybody's satisfaction is just when it was exactly that the prankster Wallace began faking giant footprints. Some sceptics believe that he was directly responsible for the footprints discovered by Gerry Crew. They allege that Wallace's company was falling behind with its work and that Ray Wallace wanted to come up with a bona fide reason for an extension to the deadline. If some of his workers quit due to a monster scare, he could plead for more time.

On the other hand, Wallace was away from the state on business when at least some of the tracks appeared. And it would be physically impossible for him to have faked all the evidence that had accumulated since 1958. Those who believe in the reality of Sasquatch are more inclined to believe Ray Wallace took to his hoaxing as a result of the events on the Bluff Creek road construction site. As an established practical joker, Wallace realized the possibilities of the events that had fallen into his lap and set out to exploit them.

Whatever the truth of Wallace's involvement, the events were significant for a number of other reasons. The fact that the newspapers and radio stations were suddenly putting out stories about Bigfoot prompted many people to step forward and give public accounts of their encounters with the creatures.

In general these added little that was new to the picture that was being built up, but they did indicate that there was far more evidence doing the rounds than a few giant footprints around a construction site. Without doubt, though, the reports also encouraged people who had encountered the creature or its footprints to come forward more readily to talk to the newspapers, or to supply information to one or other of the new breed of researchers. This contributed to the massive increase in the numbers of reports being made of the creature and the tracks it left behind.

REPORTS MULTIPLY

An early instance came from Hidden Lake in British Columbia in the summer of 1959. Mr and Mrs Bellevue were out camping in the area, as they had done several times before. One evening Mrs Bellevue wandered off in search of firewood. Then she suddenly saw a human-like figure watching her from the cover of some trees. The figure was about 6 feet (183 cm) tall and covered in reddish-brown hair. Mrs Bellevue retreated to the campsite, but decided against mentioning anything to her husband in case of ridicule. Later that night, though, she felt that it would be best if they were to leave the area. She suggested the idea and her husband replied that he had also been getting a very strong feeling that they weren't welcome. As the pair packed up next morning they heard something big, heavy and bipedal moving in the dense undergrowth nearby, although they did not see anything.

The true importance of the 1958 events, and the stories that followed them, was not realized for many years. In fact, the subject still provokes controversy among those who study the Sasquatch. First and foremost, the publicity surrounding the events opened the collective eyes of the North American public to the fact that there might be a gigantic man-like ape roaming the backwoods. As we have seen, one effect of this was that people were more willing to come forward with reports about the Sasquatch. But members of the public also began to confuse the Sasquatch with other animals. For instance, people from urban backgrounds travelling through rural areas would often see a bear and report it, in all good faith, as a Sasquatch. Their lack of familiarity with wildlife was the cause of such mistakes. These false sightings continue to bedevil research into the Sasquatch. It can take a good deal of work to distinguish between a genuine encounter and such a false report.

Glowing eyes

Far more controversial is a string of sightings of Sasquatch in areas where they had not been reported for generations and where common sense would suggest that the density of human population would mean that they should not be found.

One of the first of these came from Davis, West Virginia, in 1960. A group of young men were camping out in some woods. One of them felt a sudden dig in his ribs. Thinking it was a friend wanting his attention, he turned around. Instead of a friend he found himself looking at an 8-foot-tall (244 cm) figure covered in long, shaggy hair all over its body. The creature had enormous eyes that glowed as if with some sort of inner fire. After frightening the teenager, the beast walked off into the trees.

It was not immediately obvious from the early reports, but some researchers began to suspect that the Bigfoot that was being reported from the forests of the Eastern United States was distinct from the one being reported in the Pacific Northwest. It began to be termed the Eastern Bigfoot, as if it were a different species. As the records of sightings and encounters grew in the decades that followed, the differences between the two types of Bigfoot, or Sasquatch, would become increasingly pronounced.

Different again was the strange creature that began to be reported from Florida and the surrounding area. This soon acquired the name of Skunk Ape, both because of its offensive smell and because it appeared to be much more like an ape than a hominid.

The reports began to be made public in the early 1960s, after the Bluff Creek events had opened up the press to such stories. One important early sighting took place south of Clanton, Alabama, in 1960. The Revd E.C. Hand and half a dozen others saw an ape of some sort bounding along beside Route 31. They called Sheriff T.J. Lockhart who found two sets of tracks, one larger than the other. The larger footprints were about the size of a man's foot, with the big toe sticking out sideways, while the smaller footprints were identical in shape, but half the size.

A photo taken by a backpacker on 17 November 2005 on Silver Star Mountain: the figure vanished within seconds.

In 1962 a Kentucky farmer named Owen Powell spotted what he reported as a gorilla on his land. It was about 6 feet (183 cm) tall when it stood up on its hind legs and it was covered in black fur. In 1967 Howard Deeson of Oklahoma became almost friendly with what he thought was a chimpanzee perhaps escaped from a zoo. He left out pieces of fruit for it and watched it at fairly close range off and on for about three years. In 1968 Hamburg, in Arkansas, was the site of several fleeting sightings of a similar creature.

As with the Eastern Bigfoot, it took some time for researchers to realize that most reports coming from the southern states, and especially from Florida, were describing something that seemed to be different from the Sasquatch of the Pacific Northwest. In this case the creature seems to have been very much more like a conventional ape. The hind feet of chimpanzees, orang-utans and gorillas all have a big toe that sticks out sideways, more like a thumb. This is because they use their hind legs for grasping as well as for walking. Nor do they habitually walk on their hind feet, but instead they will walk on all fours. When they do this they curl their hands into loose fists and support themselves on their knuckles. This way of moving demands a particular kind of bone structure in the hind foot, one that allows the big toe to remain prehensile. It was to become gradually clear that the apes being seen in the damp or swampy forest lands of the southeastern states of the United States were apes of this kind, though no such creatures were recognized by science.

A Bigfoot eating red fir tree bark captured by a hidden camera in Moyie Springs, nothern Idaho.

In the immediate wake of the 1958 Bluff Creek events, however, all this lay in the future. At the time all that anyone was prepared to accept was that a large number of reports of footprints and sightings were being made.

Then, in 1961, Larry Martin reported a dramatic confrontation with a Sasquatch in the wooded hills above Alpine, Oregon. He had gone into the woods early one evening to help a friend retrieve a deer that he had shot. The two men drove up a dirt track to a spot close to the kill, then set off on foot. When they reached the spot where the deer should have been, it had gone. A clear drag mark led towards a patch of dense undergrowth so, intrigued, the two men followed. As Martin entered the bushes they were suddenly shaken with great violence by unseen hands.

Suddenly a Sasquatch came into view – it was only a few feet away. It was about 7 feet (213 cm) tall, it stood upright and it had the head and face of a gorilla, Martin later reported. He did not stay to find out more, but screamed and fled, rapidly followed by his friend. The Sasquatch gave chase with long, loping strides that thumped the ground, but the two men leapt into the car, started the engine and raced off. As he glanced in the rearview mirror, Martin saw the Sasquatch standing just a few yards behind them, watching them go.

This incident is interesting because of the light it casts on Sasquatch behaviour. First, it would seem that the Sasquatch had stumbled across the dead deer and decided to take possession of it, presumably so that it could eat the flesh. It had then dragged the deer into cover. This is the typical behaviour of an animal seeking to protect a carcass from scavengers and other predators.

When Martin and his friend approached, the Sasquatch waited until they were close to the deer, then began shaking the bushes. Again, this is fairly typical behaviour for an animal that perceives itself to be under threat. Gorillas, chimpanzees and other apes will routinely shake bushes with great violence when they want to frighten off an intruder. The performance can create an enormous amount of noise and movement for minimal effort and so it often scares off a new arrival. In this case it did not work, so the Sasquatch resorted to a personal appearance.

Interestingly, the Sasquatch did not catch up with Martin and his comrade. It seems unlikely that a 7-foot-tall (213 cm) hominid could not outpace someone under 6 feet (183 cm) tall. This raises the distinct possibility that the Sasquatch did not really want to catch the humans – perhaps it just wanted to drive them away from the disputed deer kill. Once that had been achieved, it was probably content to watch

> Suddenly a Sasquatch came into view – it was only a few feet away. It was about 7 feet (213 cm) tall, it stood upright and it had the head and face of a gorilla...

them go. Presumably it then went back to feast on the deer carcass.

In the spring of 1961 a woman walking near Bella Coola Inlet, British Columbia, had an encounter that again shed light on Sasquatch behaviour. She saw a female Sasquatch, which she could identify by its large breasts, walking along a river bank. Alongside it walked a juvenile Sasquatch, which was holding the adult by the hand. It was a very maternal and remarkably human-looking scene.

A few weeks later, in June, a Sasquatch made a dramatic visit to the isolated farm of Robert Hatfield near Fort Bragg, California. Late one evening the farm dogs began barking loudly. Hatfield went to investigate and from his front porch saw a hairy head peering over the 6 foot (183 cm) fence that surrounded the yard. Thinking it was a large bear, he went back into the house to fetch his brother-in-law Bud Jenkins, who happened to be staying.

While Jenkins fetched a torch and a rifle and his wife (Hatfield's sister) peered out into the darkness, Hatfield went back out into the yard. Hearing a noise from around the corner of the house he went to investigate and almost bumped into a hair-covered human-like figure that stood almost 8 feet (244 cm) tall. Hatfield fled, tripped and continued on his hands and knees. He dashed into the house at top speed, screaming at his sister to shut the door. She went to close the door, but it jammed while still slightly ajar. Something was holding it open with great force.

By this time Jenkins had found his rifle and was stepping past the terrified Hatfield. 'Let it through,' he told his wife. 'I'll get it.'

He lifted his rifle into the shooting position and prepared to fire at whatever it was that was about to come through the door. As the woman hesitated, the door suddenly went slack. She slammed it shut and bolted it securely. Jenkins then walked to the window to peer out into the darkness. He saw a human-like figure striding off. It stepped over a 3-foot-high (91 cm) fence without pausing and then faded out of sight into the darkness.

In July a creature approached a car that contained two teenage courting couples. It was parked in an isolated lane. The four youngsters reported that the beast bounded along on four legs and then stood up on its hind legs to peer in at them. It growled menacingly and then fled, moving and behaving rather like the creature that would later become known as the Skunk Ape. The next month, at Stoney Lake, back in British Columbia, Alex Lindstrom reported seeing a greyish-coloured Sasquatch; it was about 8 feet (244 cm) tall and it fled as soon as it spotted him.

Lurking in a graveyard

In August, John Bringsli was out picking huckleberries near Nelson, British Columbia. After parking his car he wandered off into the woods with a basket. He did not hear anything, but on looking up from his task of picking berries he saw a Sasquatch walking hesitatingly and slowly toward him. The creature stood about 8 feet (244 cm) tall and it was covered in greyish hair. At a distance of less than 50 feet (15 m), the two looked at each other for a moment in silence and then Bringsli fled for his car. The last time he saw the Sasquatch it was still close to the huckleberry bush. It was watching him leave with what seemed to be curiosity, more than anything else.

It is possible that the Sasquatch seen by Lindstrom and Bringsli were, in fact, the same creature. Grey is not a colour that is often reported among Sasquatch. What is reported, however, is that a Sasquatch, or a group of them, will be seen in an area on several occasions over a short period of time and then seem to vanish. It is as if they have arrived, spent some time in an area and then moved on.

In August an Eastern Bigfoot put in an appearance near Richmond, Indiana. This creature was reported to be about 6 feet (183 cm) tall and covered with white fur. It had glowing red eyes and was seen lurking in a graveyard. A similar creature was to be seen in November standing in a creek near Decatur, Illinois.

However, the main focus of Sasquatch activity remained in the Pacific Northwest. In August, Mrs Calhoun was prospecting with her daughter near Quesnel, British Columbia. The pair had found a stream that looked a likely spot for panning and the

With solid evidence to hand, Sasquatch hunter John Green (right) makes inquiries about sightings of Bigfoot at Easterville, Manitoba, Canada in the late 1970s.

daughter had gone back to the car to fetch a packed lunch. When Mrs Calhoun heard a noise she glanced round to see that a creature was watching her from the fringes of the forests that grew down to the stream's banks. The beast was very human in appearance, though its arms were too long in proportion to its body and it was covered in pale brown hair. Its head and shoulders were covered in longer, densely matted hair and the top of its head sloped up and back to a point, while the nose was broad and flat.

Mrs Calhoun swung her rifle up to her shoulder and covered the beast as she began to edge along the stream towards her car. The Sasquatch watched her for a few seconds and then stepped back into the undergrowth and slipped out of sight. Mrs Calhoun was convinced that it was still watching her and that it followed her to her car.

In October a man named Dutch Holler saw a Sasquatch. It was about 7 feet (213 cm) tall and it was walking casually through woodland near Spokane, Washington State. A few days later another Sasquatch was seen by Joe Gregg as he drove along a highway near Yarrow, British Columbia. It walked casually across the road in the beams of his headlights and then slipped away into the woods.

On 27 January 1963 the police at Tuolumne, California took a telephone call from a man who said that he had seen a 10-foot-tall (304 cm) hairy giant in some woodland. Sheriff Bill Huntley picked up a local tracker named Elbert Miller and went to investigate. Both men thought that the caller had probably seen a large bear, so they expected to find bear tracks. They found no bear tracks as they combed the area of woodland but they did hear a terrifying scream that sounded like a man who was in terrible agony. Wondering if the caller had been attacked by the bear, Huntley called out. He was answered by another scream, but this time from a different direction. Huntley and Miller soon concluded that there were two or more things in the forest that were circling around them, so they retreated to their car. The creatures continued to call for some time and then the cries seemed to come from further and further away until they faded into the distance.

The creature in the clearing

The Huntley-Miller incident has a place in Sasquatch research because this was the first time a Bigfoot call had been reported. Earlier witnesses had reported whistles, grunts, gurgles and even growls, but this unearthly scream was something new in 1963.

Almost exactly a month later, on 28 February, a pilot claimed that he had taken the first photographs of a Sasquatch. Lennart Strand and Alden Hoover were flying over wilderness forest land near Confidence, California, when they spotted an odd creature in a clearing. It could only be described as half-bear and half-gorilla. Strand had a camera with him, so he took some photographs. When they were developed they had been affected by camera shake, probably caused by the vibration of the light aircraft's engine. All that could be made out was a darkish blur that looked vaguely human-shaped.

In June 1963 Stan Mattson reported that when he had been walking alongside the Lewis River Canal, near Yale in Washington State, he had seen a female Sasquatch carrying a baby under its arm. As soon as he saw the creature he froze, and so escaped detection. For several minutes he watched as the Sasquatch squatted down by the canal and reached repeatedly into the water. Each time its hand was withdrawn from the water it was put into its mouth. Mattson was not close enough to see for certain, but he got the impression that the Sasquatch was catching small fish.

A woman heard her watchdogs barking first in alarm and then in fear. She peered out of the window to see what was going on. She received a terrible shock when she saw a huge, ape-like face peering back at her. The Sasquatch seemed just as surprised as she was…

Elsewhere on the Lewis River, this time near its confluence with the Columbia River in Oregon, another Sasquatch was seen. This time the witnesses, Mr and Mrs Martin Hennrich, were spotted by the creature which fled into some woodland. They reported the event to the local press, and the story was spotted by John Green. He hurried to the scene and was able to take plaster casts of the 16-inch tracks that had been left behind by the creature. This was one of the very first times that casts had been taken of footprints that could be definitely linked to one of the Sasquatch that were being reported. Previously the footprints that had been found in woods or rural areas had not been accompanied by a sighting.

When Sasquatch were seen it had either been on hard ground or it had rained soon afterwards and spoiled any prints that might have been made. It had been only conjecture that the giant footprints were being made by giant human-like creatures. This combined sighting and footprint casting finally seemed to confirm that the two phenomena were, indeed, aspects of the same enigma.

A number of reports made in the early 1960s revealed the fact that the relationship between Sasquatch and dogs was one of mutual animosity. At Toppenish in Washington State, in the spring of 1963, a woman heard her watchdogs barking first in alarm and then in fear. It was late evening and dusk was closing in, but the woman went to peer out of the window to see what was going on. She received a terrible shock when she saw a huge, ape-like face peering back at her. The Sasquatch seemed to be just as surprised as she was, because it fled. In July of the same year a Sasquatch approached the home of Gladys Herrarra, an isolated house near Satus Pass, Washington State. Again the first sign of anything unusual was the frenzied and terrified behaviour of Herrarra's pet dog.

In October 1966 the Corey homestead near Yakima, Washington State, was visited by a Sasquatch which was around 7 feet (213 cm) tall. The family dog attacked it, but the Sasquatch simply slapped it aside. When Mike Corey emerged from his house, the Sasquatch made off into the woods. Two days later the dog was found dead. It had been savagely beaten to death, presumably by the Sasquatch.

A report made to the indefatigable John Green in the summer of 1963 showed that Sasquatch were not always hostile. A man out hunting deer around Mount Shasta fell and injured his leg so badly that he could barely hobble. He was seriously alarmed when he was approached by a pale-coloured Sasquatch that stood about 8 feet (244 cm) tall. The Sasquatch watched him for a while, then came forward and picked the terrified man up and carried him to the nearest road. Because the Sasquatch did him no harm the man presumed that it was trying to help by carrying him to a road that it knew was frequented by humans.

Soon afterwards a camper named Harry Squiness had his own close encounter with a Sasquatch when camping near Anahim Lake in British Columbia. After entering his tent he had just climbed into his sleeping bag when he heard a noise outside. He sat up, whereupon the tent flap was very roughly pulled aside and what he described as a gigantic monkey face was thrust in. Squiness grabbed a torch, whereupon the creature disappeared. He followed it outside and was alarmed to see four Sasquatch all within 20 feet (6 m) of his tent. When he shouted at them all of the creatures walked off into the forest and did not return.

> He sat up, whereupon the tent flap was roughly pulled aside and what he described as a gigantic monkey face was thrust in.

In the summer of 1964 a driver spotted a Sasquatch standing beside a lay-by near Elsie, Oregon. The creature was bending down to peer through the windows of a parked station wagon. When the driver pulled up the Sasquatch fled. Inside the car was a sleeping man who had been the object of the creature's attention. Needless to say he left hurriedly when he was woken up and told what had been happening.

In July 1965 a Sasquatch was seen swimming some distance away from the shore of Princess Royal Island, British Columbia. The fisherman who saw it realized with no little apprehension that it was actually swimming for his boat, so he started up his outboard motor and sped off. At this point four more Sasquatch appeared on a nearby beach and watched him.

The sighting added swimming to the reported skills of the Sasquatch. This could have been inferred from the fact that Sasquatch had been seen on offshore islands, but it was the first time that one of these creatures was actually seen swimming. It is not generally realized that swimming is unusual among apes. Most apes cannot swim: humans and Sasquatch are among the few that can.

That autumn brought the apparent evidence that Sasquatch were not just confined to stealing dead deer from human hunters: they could actively hunt on their own account. Herb Brown was out hunting near LaPorte, California, when he saw four deer moving through the forest. Behind them came a Sasquatch that was moving very carefully and quite silently, as if it were stalking them. The creatures moved out of sight before Brown could see the result of what seemed to be a hunt.

An interesting piece of hearsay, it could not really be called evidence, surfaced at the Tollgate Restaurant in the Blue Mountains of Washington State. The owner of the establishment has an interest in Sasquatch and encourages his customers to tell him of any encounters. One customer handed over a photograph which showed a dead cougar beside a Sasquatch footprint. The customer said that he had been following a Sasquatch trail in the area when he came across the dead cougar. It had been killed by having its skull crushed by a rock. Nearby were the bones of a deer, picked clean and heavily gnawed. He concluded from this that the Sasquatch had stolen the deer kill from the cougar and when the big cat objected the creature had killed it. Unfortunately the customer did not leave his name or contact details so the story cannot be checked in any way.

The Bizarre Eastern Bigfoot

Meanwhile the Eastern Bigfoot was being seen less often than its western counterpart, but in increasingly bizarre circumstances. Lew Lister had been driving his 18-year-old future wife home. When the young couple pulled over to the side of the road that led to the girl's farmhouse home near Point Isabel in Ohio they saw an unnaturally tall human-like figure approaching over a field. The thing moved in a series of bounding leaps. Lew switched on the car's headlights to get a better look at the creature. It was tall, two-legged, and covered with yellowish blonde hair while its enormous eyes glowed a blazing orange.

As soon as the headlights came on the creature began running towards the car. Passing through a wire fence, rather than jumping over it, it then began to attack. It reached in through the open window and tried to grab Lister, but he managed to duck aside and wind up the window. The girl, meanwhile, felt mesmerized by the creature's orange eyes. After the creature curled back its lips to reveal its hideous fangs it dropped down on to all fours, snarled and vanished into thin air.

Another apparent Eastern Bigfoot attack took place on 13 September 1965. Christine van Acker, aged 17, and her mother were driving through woods near Monroe in Michigan. It was a balmy night and the pair had the car windows down. Suddenly a hulking great figure stepped out of the trees and stood in the road. It was about 7 feet (213 cm) tall and covered in dark hair. Christine, a novice driver, tried to swerve past it and accelerate, but succeeded only in stalling the car. Seconds later the creature was beside the car and reaching in. The smell was overpowering. It put a hairy hand on Christine's head and banged it against the steering wheel and then it turned and walked off as another vehicle approached.

Even more terrifying was the Bigfoot encountered by James Crabtree when out squirrel hunting near Fouke, Arkansas, in 1965. He saw some horses bolting across a field and heard what he thought was a dog howling in pain. Going to investigate, 14-year-old Crabtree found himself suddenly confronted by something that was 8 feet (244 cm) tall, human-shaped and covered with reddish hair. The beast's face was completely featureless, apart from a broad nose and masses of cascading hair. This hairy being began moving toward Crabtree with solid, lumbering steps. Crabtree raised his shotgun and blasted the creature at a range of about 25 (7.5 m) feet but the shot had no effect, so he shot again. Again, it had no effect. This time the boy lifted the gun so that its barrel was pointing at the Bigfoot's head. At a range of under 10 feet (304 cm) he pulled the trigger but still the beast came lumbering forward. Crabtree fled and got away uninjured.

> The creature was beside the car, reaching in. It put a hairy hand on Christine's head and banged it against the steering wheel…

Equally odd, though reported in all good faith, was the 7-foot-tall (213 cm) Bigfoot covered in glossy black fur that was reported to be strolling through a park in Morristown, New Jersey, on 21 May 1966.

Odd behaviour

It was not only in the Eastern States that these creatures could appear to behave oddly. In May 1967 two teenage girls spotted a Sasquatch in woods near Dalles in Oregon. It was an 8-foot-tall (244 cm) hairy man-like creature.

Their encounter was unremarkable in itself; it fitted in to what was becoming a pattern for the Pacific Northwest. When they fled the animal followed them for a short distance, then seemed to lose interest before wandering off. It was the sequel that was so unusual.

The girls told their friends about the encounter and on the following day no fewer than 12 teenagers, some armed with guns they had borrowed from their families, returned to the site of the encounter. The teenagers split up to search the woods for the Sasquatch. Dennis Taylor and Dave Churchill came across it first. They were pushing through dense undergrowth when they spotted a crouching, hairy ape-like beast in the dim light under a tree.

Although it was crouching, the creature was at least 7 feet (213 cm) tall. It began to stand up, whereupon Churchill shot it in the chest with both barrels of his 12-gauge shotgun, at a range of under 20 feet (6 m). The impact of the blast knocked the creature over but it then stood up and calmly walked off as if uninjured.

Bullet-proof wonders

These bizarre encounters were mostly with the Eastern Bigfoot, though at this date the creature was not yet recognized as being distinct from the Pacific Northwest Sasquatch. Researchers who believed in the reality of a hominid ape that was native to North America tended to look askance at these encounters. The aggressive, bullet-proof wonders that were able to vanish into thin air simply did not fit into the pattern of a real creature that the researchers were trying to build up. Some of them ignored the wilder reports altogether, others included the incidents in their writings but glossed over the more inexplicable features.

On the other hand the sceptics, who thought that the entire Bigfoot–Sasquatch enigma was a fraud or a hallucination, seized on these bizarre reports with tremendous enthusiasm. They could use them to portray the entire story as the stuff of delusion, nonsense and fraud.

By the summer of 1967 the world outside the Pacific Northwest had been aware of the Sasquatch for nine years. What had begun as an intriguing mystery relating to the gigantic footprints that had been found around a road construction site had mushroomed dramatically. Hundreds of people had reported finding footprints, seeing man-apes in the forests and having encounters with beasts that seemed to have come straight out of a horror movie. Some investigators were convinced that the Sasquatch was a real creature, others were giving up in despair because of the sensational and otherworldly aspects of the phenomenon.

Meanwhile, back in the Pacific Northwest a temporarily unemployed rodeo rider was setting out on a journey that would turn the world of cryptozoology upside down. Roger Patterson was heading to Bluff Creek with a movie camera and what he recorded continues to dominate all discussion of the Sasquatch to this day.

3 Shooting a Sasquatch

The Patterson Film

The short cine film shot by Roger Patterson on 20 October 1967 in the Bluff Creek area of northern California remains the most important single piece of evidence for the existence of a real upright-walking hominid ape that was living wild in North America. Some might argue that the cumulative evidence of footprints, sightings and other evidence is even more persuasive, but the Patterson movie remains one of the most famous and controversial 'proofs' of the existence of cryptids (animals unrecognized by science).

Patterson and his companion that day, Bob Gimlin, have been hailed as heroes and condemned as crooks. They have been praised for their skill at tracking down a Sasquatch or dismissed as lucky amateurs, even by those who now believe the film is genuine. Those who are convinced that the film is a fake have either condemned Patterson and Gimlin as hoaxers and frauds or written them off as the gullible instruments of a fraud perpetrated by others.

The Sasquatch glances back in this famous still from the Patterson Film.

Given the massive amounts of controversy that still surround the film, it is interesting to look not only at the film itself, and what it seems to show, but also at the background to it. Details of events surrounding the film are often passed over but they can shed much-needed light on the events of that autumnal day.

In 1967 Roger Patterson was a rodeo rider living at Yakima, Washington, but because work was intermittent he did odd jobs for his brother-in-law, Al DeAtley. Patterson was also very interested in the Sasquatch enigma. He seems to have missed the excitement that centred around the events of 1958 at the Bluff Creek road works, but in 1964 he read an article by Ivan T. Sanderson. In that article, Sanderson compared the evidence for Sasquatch with that for the Yeti of the Himalayas. At this date, Sanderson was referring to all such supposed cryptid apes as ABSM (Abominable Snow Men), the translation of one of the Nepalese names for the Yeti. Patterson became very interested in the idea that there might be an American Abominable Snow Man living near his own home. As a result, he spent some of his spare time collecting reports, interviewing witnesses and casting footprints.

On some of these trips he was accompanied by a friend named Bob Gimlin. Gimlin was a part-time horse breeder, part-time rodeo rider and occasional construction worker. He was also partly descended from the Yakama, and like all First Nations people, he had heard stories about the hairy man-apes all his life – but did not really take them very seriously. He did, however, enjoy the outdoors and was happy to travel the wilderness areas with his friend Patterson when he had nothing better to do.

The Sasquatch walks off into the trees, setting off a worlwide debate about whether the film is genuine.

In 1966 Patterson pulled all his material together in a book entitled *Do Abominable Snowmen of America Really Exist?* It sold fairly well locally, but did not make much of a profit. Patterson then had the idea of making a documentary film about these mystery apes, although he did not really know much about the television business, and did not even own a camera. He decided to get some footage of witness interviews and footprints using a camera hired from a camera shop in Yakima and then try to get somebody from the TV business interested in the idea.

Into the wilderness

In early October, Patterson got a call from one of his contacts in the growing community of Sasquatch investigators, a man from Willow Creek in California called Al Hodgson. Hodgson told him that some excellent new tracks had been found in the Blue Creek Mountain area. They were being studied by John Green and René Dahinden. It was thought that one set of very large footprints had been made by a big male, a smaller set of footprints by a female and a third, much smaller set of prints by a juvenile.

Patterson contacted Gimlin, who agreed to go along. This was important because Gimlin had a truck and a horse van that allowed the pair to take horses with them and then ride into the wilderness. Without Gimlin, Patterson would have been on foot and unable to cover so much ground.

The pair arrived on 6 October, by which time heavy rains had washed away the tracks that Patterson had hoped to film. They decided to stay, though, having come prepared for a two-week visit. The pair would drive to a likely area, make camp and then take to their horses and spend the day riding about looking for footprints or other signs of Sasquatch.

On 20 October they were camped in the Bluff Creek area. They spent the morning riding separately, then around noon joined up to explore a particularly rugged and remote region centred around a canyon. Thinking that they might stay out overnight, the men loaded a packhorse. Patterson rode in front and Gimlin followed up behind,

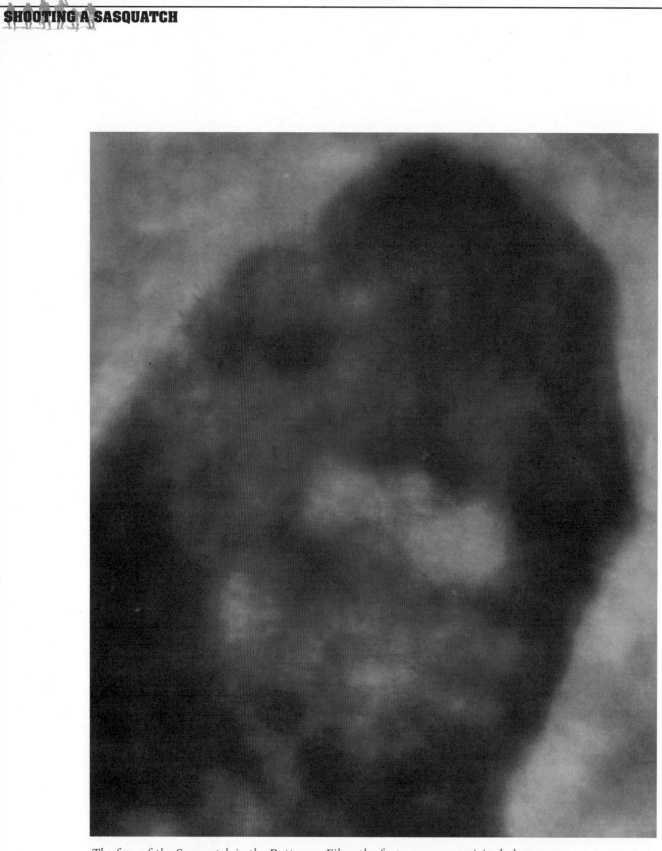

The face of the Sasquatch in the Patterson Film: the features are suprisingly human.

leading the animal. Both men were armed, but it was Patterson who had the cine camera in his saddlebags.

According to Patterson and Gimlin they had been riding for some hours when they reached a pile of fallen trees and broken logs that had been left there by a flood back in

1964. The obstruction blocked their view up the canyon, but also masked them from the sight of anything beyond it. As they came around the log jam they saw a Sasquatch beside the creek about 80 feet (24.5 m) from them. The creature saw them at the same time and it stood up abruptly and stared at them.

At this point Patterson's horse began bucking and trying to turn around. Patterson grabbed the cine camera from the saddlebag, then sprang down from the horse which bolted off downstream. Gimlin's horse was older and more placid, but even so it began to get agitated. When the Sasquatch began to walk off along the creek bank, heading for the dense forests that lined the canyon. Patterson got the cine-camera working and yelled out, 'Cover me,' to Gimlin. At this, Gimlin pulled out his rifle, thereby letting go of the pack horse, which headed off downstream after Patterson's mount.

Close encounter

Patterson was now running forward with the camera to his eye, trying to keep the Sasquatch in shot. He did not see a sudden rise in the ground so he tripped and fell. The Sasquatch turned to stare at him. Fearing the creature might attack, Gimlin rode over to the creek, dismounted and aimed his rifle at the Sasquatch, now only about 60 feet (18 m) away. Scrambling back to his feet Patterson re-focused the camera on the Sasquatch, which was by now walking off again. The creature turned again to look at the two men, but did not break its stride as it had done before. It continued to walk away and then passed around a bend in the canyon. That was when Patterson ran out of film, but the two men could still hear the creature moving off. It seemed to be running quite fast.

Gimlin and Patterson hurriedly discussed the situation. Gimlin thought the creature had been approaching 7 feet (213 cm) tall and had weighed around 300 pounds. Patterson thought it had been a foot taller and much heavier. Both men had noticed that the creature had breasts and concluded that it was a female.

Gimlin wanted to push on up the creek in pursuit of the creature, but Patterson refused. His rifle was still on his horse, and he did not know where that had got to. Patterson pointed out that they had come out looking for a family group of Sasquatch, but had seen only one female. The much larger male might be nearby and it would probably not be as timid as the female had been when it saw the humans, especially if it thought that they might be threatening its mate and its young.

The two men headed back downstream, caught the two horses which had stopped only a short distance away and returned to the site of the encounter. After tying the packhorse up they headed off upstream, taking care not to disturb the Sasquatch tracks. They then followed the tracks for about 600 yards. The trail turned away from the creek and into the wooded slopes of the canyon, at which point they probed just far enough to confirm that the creature had headed uphill, then stopped. Again, Gimlin wanted to push on, but Patterson did not. He was still nervous about the big male and the ability of their rifles to stop such a big beast. Moreover, he wanted to get back to the footprints.

By this time it was late afternoon and dusk would soon close in. The weather did not look too promising and Patterson was keen to carry on filming and cast the tracks before night closed in. With a new film in the camera, he took extensive shots of the Sasquatch tracks and then cast the clearest footprints that he could find. Other good prints were covered over with bark and twigs to protect them from the threatening rain.

Patterson and Gimlin rode back to their camp, cared for the horses and then climbed

Bob Gimlin (left) and Roger Patterson compare casts of the Bigfoot prints they found.

into the truck. They drove to Eureka to post the precious movie film off for processing. Patterson was worried that he might not have got much useable film because he had been running for part of the time and then had fallen to his knees. On the way back to camp they stopped off to see Al Hodgson and they told him about the day's events. Hodgson later recalled that although Patterson was highly excited he was fretting about how good the film would prove to be. The three men agreed that Hodgson should phone Green and Dahinden to tell them about the events while Patterson and Gimlin went back to camp.

Word spread quickly among Sasquatch researchers. One of those to hear about Patterson's movie before it had been developed was Bob Titmus. He decided to travel to the scene of the encounter to study the tracks. By this time Titmus had become a firm believer in the reality of Sasquatch. Although he had been a sceptic when he was initially involved in 1958 he now claimed to have seen one of the creatures for himself. He arrived at the narrow canyon site eight days after the encounter. There had been a shower of rain in the meantime but although this had erased some detail from the footprints the main features were still clear.

Titmus took some casts of the prints that Gimlin had covered over with bark and twigs to protect them from the rain. They showed the Sasquatch moving exactly as Patterson and Gimlin had claimed. Starting from the creek, the creature had gone upstream and then around the canyon corner before disappearing into the trees. He also measured the stride length and other details, confirming that the stride length increased markedly once the Sasquatch had been out of sight of the men. He measured the depth of the Sasquatch tracks at one point at 1.25 inches. He then measured his brother-in-law's footprints at the same point and they were 0.25 inches deep. His brother in law weighed 200 pounds, so Titmus concluded that the Sasquatch must have weighed around 600 pounds.

He then looked at the tracks of the horses and men. These were more confused, because the men and the horses had moved back and forth. He was able to pick out Patterson's route while he had been filming, including his knee marks where he had fallen.

Titmus then followed the Sasquatch tracks into the forest, well beyond the point where Patterson and Gimlin had given up the chase. The Sasquatch had

> The creature had gone upstream and then around the canyon corner before disappearing into the trees.

actually turned round to go back down the canyon. After a few hundred feet it had stopped and then sat down. Looking back downhill, Titmus realised that he had an uninterrupted view of the scene of the encounter. The Sasquatch must have sat here watching Patterson and Gimlin as they caught their horses, cast the footprints and shot their film of the scene. It had then got up and walked off uphill and deeper into the forest. Titmus then returned to the scene of the encounter and backtracked the Sasquatch.

When Patterson and Gimlet had first seen it, the Sasquatch had just crossed the creek and paused – perhaps to drink. On the other side of the creek, the tracks showed that the Sasquatch had come down from the forested mountain. Titmus followed them for over a quarter of a mile before he lost them.

Some months later the site was visited by John Green. He brought with him a student by the name of Jim McClarin who, at 6 feet 5 inches (198 cm), was the tallest man he could talk into accompanying him. Green stood where Patterson had been standing after his fall and filmed McClarin following the route of the Sasquatch. The movie would in due course reveal much, including the Sasquatch's height of around 7 feet 4 inches (223 cm), but the most immediate revelation was that the creature had stepped up a 30-inch-high bank without breaking its stride.

Before moving on to look at the film in detail, it is worth pointing out a few features of the events as they had unfolded. First, Patterson was not a rich man nor was he one of the mainstream researchers working on the Sasquatch enigma. His resources were very limited and he was not able to access all of the information that was currently available. If, as many people have alleged, he faked the whole event then he must have done so on a shoestring budget and without being certain that his hoaxed figure would match what other researchers knew of the elusive creature.

Second, Patterson had been excitedly telling Hodgson about the encounter before the film had been developed. Most of those who have been guilty of faking photos of UFOs and other enigmas have waited until they have produced a good fake before telling anyone about their alleged encounter with the unknown.

Third, the Titmus visit showed that whatever made the Sasquatch tracks had walked for over 600 yards through the forest and then downhill to the creek, crossed the creek and walked along the canyon before turning back into the forest and moving uphill for at least another 300 yards. This sort of behaviour seems to have been very similar to that of a real wild creature. If the film had been a fake, it is much more likely that the tracks would have started and finished on the canyon floor where the filming took place. Of course, a fraudster might well think that laying extra prints would add credibility to the fake film and so take the trouble to make the false trail. But neither Patterson nor Gimlin tried to persuade anyone to go to look for these tracks, as they presumably would have done if they had spent time making them. It was only because Titmus went to the site on his own initiative that he found the tracks.

Fourth, so far as is known only Patterson and Gimlin knew where they were riding that day. If a third party had been playing a trick on them, that person would have needed to know where to go to act the part of a Sasquatch.

Guarded reaction

Moreover, Gimlin was a crack shot and, unlike Patterson, was not known to anyone in the circle of Sasquatch researchers. He might have taken it into his head to open fire and at such a short range would have almost certainly hit his target. Anyone prancing about in a monkey suit would have been running the very real risk of meeting an early death.

Green and Dahinden were on hand when the film came back from the developers. When it was viewed, the film showed exactly what Patterson and Gimlin had said it would. The film was quickly copied, and the original stored in a bank vault for safekeeping. Green arranged for the movie to be shown to a panel of invited scientists at the University of British Columbia because none of the local institutions in the United States were willing to become linked to Sasquatch research. The reaction of the dozen or so scientists who did turn up was extremely guarded. Dr Ian McTaggart-Cowan, the Dean of the University of British Columbia and a zoologist, was enigmatic.

'The more a thing deviates from the known, the better the proof of its existence must be.'

Don Abbott, an anthropologist at the Provincial Museum of British Columbia, was equally cautious.

'It is about as hard to believe the film is faked as it is to admit that such a creature really lives. If there is a chance to follow up scientifically, my curiosity is such that I'd want to go along with it. Like most scientists, however, I'm not ready to put my reputation on the line until something concrete shows up – something like bones or a skull.'

Frank Beebe, a well-known Vancouver naturalist, made the following statement:

'I'm not convinced, but I think the film is genuine. From a scientific standpoint, one of the hardest facts to go against is that there is no evidence anywhere in the continent of ape evolution.'

Life magazine was contacted and on the strength of the scientists in British Columbia not dismissing the film outright arranged for it to be shown in New York at the American Museum of Natural History. Unlike British Columbia, Patterson and Green were not allowed in the room while the expert scientists watched the film and studied enlarged individual frames. Nor were they allowed to take part in the press conference that followed. The New York scientists announced that in their view the film was a fake and the whole Sasquatch business was a colossal hoax. They prudently stopped short of actually accusing Patterson of faking the film himself – though that was the clear impression given to the journalists. The reasoning behind the verdict had nothing to do with the film itself, but rested on the grounds that it was impossible for there to be an unknown hominid ape in North America. And since that was impossible, it followed that the film had to be a fake.

That damning verdict effectively killed the story for the mainstream media. *Life* magazine dropped the story. *Argosy* and *Reader's Digest* both ran short articles on the film, but then they too lost interest.

At this point Gimlin dropped out of the affair. He had never really been that interested in the Sasquatch and he had a living to earn. Apart from one interview with a Vancouver radio station in November 1967 he has not since been involved. Whenever he has spoken on the subject, however, he has always insisted that the film is genuine, that he and Patterson really did encounter and film a Sasquatch and that the Sasquatch is real. Until the day of his death Patterson also firmly defended the validity of the film.

Although the scientific establishment and the mainstream media had lost interest in the

Patterson film, the growing circle of Sasquatch investigators had not. The general consensus among those who viewed the film was that it showed a creature that conformed to the descriptions given by witnesses who had encountered a Sasquatch. The question then resolved itself into whether the subject of the movie was a real Sasquatch or a fake that had been concocted to match the descriptions given by earlier eyewitnesses.

Among the first experts to be consulted were the Disney movie studios, world leaders in animatronics and all aspects of animation in the late 1960s. They studied the film and confidently ruled out any form of animation or 'special effects', effectively ruling out any visual trickery. The film showed a real figure moving in real time in a real place. Given the limitations of special effects in 1967 this verdict has never been questioned. That left only two alternatives. Either the figure was a Sasquatch or it was a man in a suit. The figure had by this time acquired the nickname of 'Patty' among researchers.

Walk like a man

One of the main early objections raised to the gait of Patty is that it resembles that of a man, not that of a woman. But the creature is very clearly a female with large breasts. It is true that Patty walks with a very masculine stride, but that does not necessarily mean that the creature is not female. The only known upright walking ape is the human. Walking styles are different in male and female humans because female hips are wider than those of a male. The reason for this is that the large brain of a human baby needs a large skull to accommodate it. Were it not for this large head, the hips of the female would not need to be wider than those of the male and so the two sexes would have a similar gait. The Sasquatch does not seem to be any more intelligent than a gorilla or a chimpanzee and witnesses do not describe a large-brained skull. This indicates that the skull of the baby Sasquatch is more in proportion to that of a baby gorilla than a baby human so the female Sasquatch would not need to have wide hips. The apparently masculine walk of Patty would, therefore, be entirely consistent with the likely hip structure of a female Sasquatch.

Dahinden then contacted a British professor of biomechanics called Don Grieve. His task was to compare the limb proportions and movements of the figure in the film to those of a human. If the figure was a human in a hairy outfit this would show it up.

Grieve began with the limb proportions and quickly concluded that 'Patty' had leg to body proportions similar to those of a man. The arms, however, were different. They were longer than those of a human and the elbow was lower down. The proportions of the arm have come in for much study because they seem to point to a clear difference between the Sasquatch and a human. The ratio between a human leg and arm is about

Russian snowman hunter Igor Bourtsev with the cast of a print he found in Tadzhikistan in 1979.

10:7; that of the creature in the Patterson film is more like 10:9.

Grieve then turned to the speed of the walk, the length of the stride and the angles formed by the thighs and the knees as the creature moved. It was clear from these that the way in which Patty walked was very different from a normal human walk. In particular the creature did not at any time lock its knees into a straight line, something which all humans do. This did not mean that the figure was not a man walking in a deliberately unusual manner. Grieve then did more calculations and came back with a query: 'At what speed in frames per second (fps) had the film been shot?'

The question was crucial. If the film had been shot at 24 fps or more, then a human male could have managed to mimic the walking style with a bit of effort. But if the film had been shot at a slower speed, no human could have moved his legs in the manner shown.

Patterson had already been asked this question by researchers trying to determine Patty's speed. He had replied that he usually set the cine camera at 24 fps but when he had reloaded the film to shoot the tracks after the sighting he had noticed that the camera was set to 16 fps.

Planet of the Apes *(1968): some say the Patterson Film featured a human in a special-effects suit.*

Perhaps it had been jolted out of its usual setting when he had stumbled, or when the camera had been bounced about in the saddlebags of his horse when it had become frightened, but he could not be certain. There was an added complication in that the model of camera that Patterson had used was not entirely reliable. Kodak, who made it, allowed for a 10 per cent margin of error on fps speed. So if set at 24 fps, the camera might actually be running at anything between 21.6 and 26.4 fps.

It was a Soviet researcher named Igor Bourtsev who found the answer. He noted that the start of the movie showed a series of up and down shudders. It was at this point that Patterson claimed that he had been running toward the Sasquatch so Bourtsev thought that the shudders might have been caused by Patterson's feet hitting the ground. At 24 fps the shudders indicated that Patterson had been taking 6 steps per second, but at 16 fps they indicated that he was taking four steps per second. When running it is simply impossible for a human to take more than five steps per second. This indicated very strongly that the actual fps speed of the film in the camera had been between 14 and 18. According to Grieve that ruled out a man in a fur suit.

Another objection that was raised to the creature in the Patterson film, and to Sasquatch in general, was that the alleged animal showed an odd mixture of ape-like and human-like features. Given the state of knowledge about hominid evolution in the later 1960s this was a valid criticism. If the Sasquatch does exist it should be a side branch of either human or great ape evolution. In the 1960s it seemed inconceivable that a great ape could walk upright, or that a primitive human would have an ape's head. Since then a great deal more has been learned about the evolution of both apes and humans. Although there is still no obvious ancestral line that could lead to a creature such as the Sasquatch, we are now aware that the evolutionary trees of the two lines were a lot more complex than previously thought. The odd mixture of ape and human features no longer appears as unlikely as it once did.

> Less than 18 months after the Patterson film was shot rumours began to filter out of the Hollywood movie industry. It was being said that Patty was a man wearing a suit produced by a special effects and make-up artist of great fame.

Less than 18 months after the Patterson film was shot rumours began to filter out of the Hollywood movie industry. It was being said that Patty was a man wearing a suit produced by a special effects and make-up artist of great fame. Contemporary reports did not name the man involved, but it was an open secret in Hollywood that he was John Chambers. Chambers worked on a vast number of projects from the 1950s to the 1970s, both in television and the movies. The project of most relevance to the Patterson film was the movie *Planet of the Apes*, released in 1968. Chambers had been responsible for the make-up and the outfits worn by the upright walking apes.

The story linking Chambers to the Patterson movie circulated widely in Hollywood. It was one of those odd secrets that everyone in a fairly closed industry knows about and delights in revealing to outsiders to demonstrate their inside knowledge. As such it cropped up in newspapers from time to time. Chambers did not confirm or deny the reports, he just smiled knowingly. In fact the tale did the career of John Chambers no end of good. In 1971 he even worked on a film about a homicidal Bigfoot terrorising a group of attractive students. The Bigfoot in this movie, *Schlock*, is oddly not as realistic as the one in the Patterson film.

The story was finally laid to rest by Chambers himself in 1997 after his retirement from the movie business. He gave an interview in which he denied knowing anything about Patterson, Gimlin or their film until long after it was taken. 'I was good,' Chambers said of his make-up talents in relation to the Patterson film, 'but I was never that good.'

Meanwhile Dr Grover Krantz and others had been studying the Patterson film with the aim of deducing the size and measurements of the creature that it showed. There were two basic starting points for the work. The first was the film shot by John Green of Jim McClarin following the route of the Sasquatch. Comparisons were made between McClarin's known height and various objects in Green's film, such as tree stumps and fallen logs, and then these were cross-referenced back to the original film. The other was a couple of frames in the footage where the soles of one of the Sasquatch's feet are shown clearly. The footprints cast by Patterson and Titmus gave the size of the feet, which allowed the size of the creature to be scaled up from the image of the sole of the foot.

> The footprints cast by Patterson and Titmus gave the size of the feet, which allowed the size of the creature to be scaled up from the image of the sole of the foot.

Although there are some slight differences of opinion among the various researchers, the overall picture that has emerged from these computations is clear. The creature is, give or take an inch, 7 feet 4 inches tall (223 cm). This is not far off what Patterson thought at the time. The chest circumference of the creature is around 50 inches (127 cm), and the circumference of the hips is about the same. In fact, the entire body of the creature is remarkably straight, showing none of the curves in and out that are more typical of human bodies. This would indicate that the creature was much more massive than a human of the same height would be. A weight of around 700 pounds would not be impossible.

The head of Patty in the film is consistent with other eyewitness reports. The jaw is heavy and it projects further forward than that of a human, but not so much as that of a gorilla. The creature's face is fairly deep and is dominated by a flattened nose and heavy ridges over the eyes, while the top of the head slopes back sharply from the eye ridges to reach a peaked crest near the back. There are no visible ears. Overall it is part way between the head of a human and that of a large ape.

The peak on the back of the head could be explained in two different ways. On the one hand it may be formed of stiff, upright hairs that form a mane. Some eyewitnesses have said that the hair on the head of the Sasquatch they encountered was longer than elsewhere. Indeed in a few frames of the Patterson film the peak does seem to bounce as it it were made of hair, but this movement is not very clear. On the other hand it might be made of muscles attached to a crest of bone sticking up from the centre of the skull. Gorillas have this feature, known as a sagittal crest, in exaggerated form. The purpose of a sagittal crest is to provide attachment for jaw muscles too powerful to be accommodated on a smooth skull top, such as that possessed by humans.

This head is mounted on a short neck that is so thick and muscled that the head seems to merge directly into the shoulders. Other eyewitnesses have commented that the creatures that they saw did not seem to have a neck, and this is probably what they meant. The arrangement of muscles that would give this impression would be associated with a heavy skull equipped with heavy jaws.

Taken altogether these features of Patty would indicate that it has large teeth set in massive jaws that are worked by very powerful jaw muscles. The brain case would be much smaller than that of a human, but it may be relatively larger than that of a gorilla. The fact that the face is flatter than that of the otherwise broadly similar gorilla or chimpanzee could be explained as an adaptation to the creature's upright stance.

Muscle movement

Another feature of the creature in the film that has come in for much study is the apparent movement of the muscles under the skin. At several points in the film the skin bulges or slackens in apparent response to the muscles. The movement of these muscles is entirely consistent with what would happen when real muscles flex and relax at the different stages of a stride. In other words, they are anatomically correct.

Some researchers have concluded that these muscle movements show that there is muscle tissue working directly underneath the skin. Because no human has the massively wide body nor the thick limbs of Patty they maintain that the creature is a genuine animal that exists exactly as it appears. This does not quite follow. Even in 1967 it was possible to fake muscle movement beneath false skin by the use of carefully shaped and cunningly positioned balloons inflated by compressed air. However, such devices were only used on fake limbs that were not attached to a real body. Quite how a person inside a monkey suit could have operated such devices while walking along has never been satisfactorily explained, but that does not mean that it was not done.

Taken as a whole, the various studies of the Patterson film and its contents produce an intriguing series of conclusions. First, the object being filmed is quite clearly really there: it is not a special effect that was added on later. Second, the appearance of the creature is entirely consistent with everything that eyewitnesses have reported about the Sasquatch either before or since. Third, it is very unlikely, but not entirely impossible, for the moving figure to be a human male in a cleverly wrought suit. Even today the manufacture of a suit that was able to move and act like the creature in Patterson's film would be a very long and costly operation. Back in 1967 it is doubtful if such a suit could have been made. Even if it were possible, it would have cost a vast amount of money and would have required a remarkable scale of technical skill and ability.

Given that Roger Patterson was an out-of-work rodeo rider it is obviously impossible for him to have either made such a suit himself or paid somebody else to do it. There remains the possibility that somebody else was involved, either in collaboration with Patterson or playing a hoax on him. Nobody has ever come forward to take the credit for that role. The most widely discussed candidate, John Chambers, ruled himself out.

In 1999 a lawyer based in Washington State announced that he had a client who claimed to have donned a monkey suit and walked up the creek for Patterson to film. The client apparently passed a lie detector test. But he backed out of a news conference at the last minute after issuing a statement, through the same lawyer, that he was trying to negotiate a fee with a national newspaper for an exclusive interview. The mystery man has not been heard from again.

But despite its great fame and the huge amount of attention that has been lavished upon it, the Patterson film is not the only moving film that appears to show a Sasquatch. In 1995 a second film emerged that was to become known as the Redwoods Footage. It has an apparent Sasquatch in view for only 25 seconds and is not very clear, having been shot at night by the light of a vehicle's headlights in conditions of light rain.

The Redwoods Footage

The film was taken by a professional videographer named Craig Miller on Walker Road in Jedediah Smith Redwoods State Park in northern California, a site that is only 30 miles from the location of the Patterson encounter. Miller had spent 28 August 1995 out in the woods filming a television show about the lifestyle of a Playboy model named Anna-Marie Goddard, who had gained fame as the magazine's 40th anniversary 'Playmate of the Month'. The film crew and team were being driven back to their hotel by Colin Goddard, Anna-Marie's husband.

As they came round a corner, Goddard spotted a hairy human-like figure crossing the road in front of the vehicle. It was perhaps 8 feet (244 cm) tall. He called out to the team behind him and Miller happened to have his video camera in his hand. Hurriedly scrambling forward, he caught a short section of video. It showed the creature move off the highway and then turn to face the approaching small coach before it darted off into the undergrowth.

When it first emerged, the film was dubbed the 'Playmate Footage', but the name was quickly dropped when it became clear that this frivolous tag would make it even less likely to be taken seriously by scientists. In the event, the very fact that Ms Goddard had been present ensured that many researchers thought that the footage might be no more than a publicity stunt for the model. She has consistently denied this, as have the other people present at the encounter.

The creature in the video is about 30 yards away when the film begins. Goddard brakes to a halt as the creature walks in front of the vehicle at a distance of about five yards, passing through the headlight beams as it does so. He chooses that moment to switch the lights to full beam, thereby illuminating the figure clearly. The creature raises an arm to shield its eyes, then walks off to the side of the road before turning to stare at the camera. It then strides off into the trees and is lost from view.

Given the poor visibility of the rainy night it is hardly surprising that the video is of rather poor quality. However, because it was on video tape the footage was easy to digitize and

A forested slope in this mock-up of a Sasquatch's typical environment, one which would fit perfectly with its nomadic lifestyle.

then enhance through a variety of formats. This work was undertaken under the direction of Dr Jeff Meldrum, a professor of anatomy with an interest in the Sasquatch. It revealed a number of interesting features that were not readily apparent in the original video.

The size of the creature could now be deduced by comparing the footage with the measurements of trees and other objects at the site of the encounter. This suggested that its height was within the range of 6 feet 4 inches (193 cm) to 7 feet 2 inches (215 cm). The enhancement also showed that the creature was very similar to the Sasquatch in the Patterson film, except that it lacked breasts and seemed to be much shaggier, with especially long hair around the head and neck.

As the legs moved there appeared to be a patch of muscle moving beneath the skin on the buttock, which corresponds to the main muscle that pulls the leg back. An object can also be seen sticking out from the front of the body, just below the waist. The curved object is not very clear, but Meldrum theorized that it might be the animal's penis. Some male apes are known to display their penis as a signal of dominance or confidence when confronted by a threat or a rival.

Impressive though the Redwoods Footage is in many ways, the poor quality of the video means that some have dismissed it as a hoax. There is simply not enough detail available to be able to rule out the possibility of the creature being a human in a disguise. Some researchers also feel that some of the people involved might have had access to special effects skills, in view of their connection to the TV industry.

The Memorial Day Footage

The following year another video of what might have been a Sasquatch was taken. Because it was shot on 26 May it has become known as the Memorial Day footage. Owen Pate, his wife and five friends were on a camping trip in the Paysaten Wilderness Area, Washington State. From their camp site, Pate and his wife saw a strange figure standing next to a bush on the edge of some woodland about 75 yards away. The figure turned to look at them, then moved off back into the cover of the woods. Mrs Pate went to get their video camera while Pate and the others discussed what they had seen. Some thought it had been a Bigfoot, others were not sure.

A few minutes later the figure reappeared about 100 yards from its first position. It then ran across the open hillside, behind a small hillock and into another stretch of woodland. A total of 22 seconds of the video shot by Mrs Pate contains images of the figure.

The video was reported to researchers and underwent the usual enhancement procedures. The figure was so far away that it is impossible to see any real detail, other than its silhouette. Disappointing though this was, it did reveal an interesting feature. When first seen, the creature was swinging only one arm as it ran; the other seemed to be holding something. After passing the hillock it seemed to be taller than before. Further digital enhancement seemed to show that the figure had, in fact, put something on to its shoulder.

It has been suggested, though the video is so indistinct that it is impossible to be

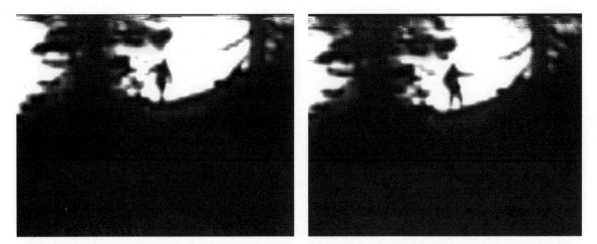

Two stills from the Memorial Day Footage (1996): the figure is thought to be a female Bigfoot.

certain, that the video shows a mother Sasquatch and its baby. At first the baby is held in one arm, pressed against the mother's body. The baby is then hoisted up on to the adult's shoulders.

Further investigations at the site seemed to show that the the initial figure was under 6 feet (183 cm) tall at first, its height then increasing by about 6 inches (15 cm). It was seen to be running as it moved. When a man set off to follow the identical route he found that he could easily cover the ground in the same time as the figure. There has never been any suggestion that the Pates or their friends faked the film, but at the same time the resolution is so poor that it is impossible to be certain what it shows.

The Freeman Footage

Much clearer, though still not as well defined as the Patterson film, was a movie shot by forestry worker Paul Freeman in 1994. According to his own account, Freeman had seen an 8-foot-tall (244 cm) Bigfoot on 10 June 1982 when working in forests near Walla Walla, Washington State. When he told his workmates about the encounter, he had come in for a lot of teasing and, at times, boisterous horseplay. As a result he began carrying a movie camera to work. In later years he updated to a video camera.

Thus it was that he was carrying a video camera when he spotted a line of Bigfoot tracks in woodland in the Blue Mountains area. Freeman measured a few footprints to gauge their size and stride length, then got out his camera and began filming the track as he followed it. He then heard movement in the undergrowth ahead of him and lifted up the camera just in time to catch a short glimpse of a tall, hairy human-like figure walking across the path that he had been following. The figure turned to glance at him, then slipped into the brush and out of sight. Freeman advanced along the path with his camera still running. The apparent Bigfoot was then seen again some distance off and Freeman moved the camera to remain focused on it. As the Bigfoot was walking away it bent down to pick something up before striding off to be lost from view in the woodland. As with other video footage, the Freeman Footage, as the film has become known, was of relatively poor quality but could be subjected to digital enhancements.

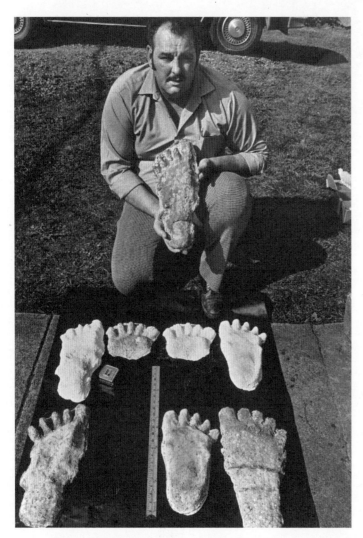

Roger Freeman with some of his footprint casts. The fact that he found so many produced much scepticism.

The figure in the video seems to be a fairly typical Sasquatch creature that is moving with a purposeful stride. The object that it bends down to pick up is poorly defined, but some viewers think that it might be a juvenile Sasquatch.

Generally, however, the distance of the subject from the camera, and a lack of definition, makes this a difficult video to extract much information from. Dr Esteban Sarmiento, a functional anatomist at the American Museum of Natural History, studied the video but was unable to form any firm conclusions about it.

F for fake?

Freeman proved to be almost as controversial a figure in Sasquatch research circles as Ray Wallace had been a generation earlier. On the credit side, he produced a large number of footprint casts, as well as the Freeman Footage video, and collected a large number of eyewitness accounts. There can be no doubting the amount of time he spent out in the forests looking for Sasquatch evidence, nor the contribution that he made to Sasquatch studies.

However the very fact that Freeman found so many tracks and other evidence, while others were much less successful, made some researchers suspicious. When a few of the tracks that he had discovered were found to have features that indicated that they might have been fakes, suspicions deepened. René Dahinden and Bob Titmus thought Freeman was simply a hoaxer seeking attention, but others were unconvinced. To the day of his death in 2003, Freeman maintained that the video footage he shot was genuine, though even he accepted that some of the footprints he had discovered may have been faked by some unidentified third party.

The Manitoba Footage

On 16 April 2005 a new film of what appears to be a Sasquatch was taken and it soon became known as the Manitoba Footage. It was shot at the Norway House ferry on the banks of the Nelson River by Bobby Clarke, who operated the ferry. The location was astonishingly remote: it was almost 50 miles (80 km) from the nearest settlement and was set amid a mature coniferous forest. According to Clarke he first noticed a strange figure on the far bank of the river. At first he thought it might be a fur trapper, but on looking more closely he realized that the figure was covered in fur. Having a video camera to hand, he filmed it.

He later showed the video to his family, who took a copy and showed it to friends. Word slowly leaked out and the video was eventually aired on ACA television. Despite the hype that it received, the Manitoba Footage did not show much detail of the figure. Like so many other short excerpts of video or film that have appeared over the years, the Manitoba Footage proved to be interesting and mysterious. The other videos include The Marble Mountains Footage, The Lembo Lake Film, Bob Dagle's Surveillance Clips and Keating's White Creature.

All of them, however, are of low technical quality and show little more than a blurred or indistinct figure that looks a bit like a Sasquatch. None of them comes even close to the Patterson film in terms of quality, lighting or subject clarity. If the Patterson film has failed to convince sceptics or scientists, then subsequent movies and videos have even less chance of convincing the scientific world of the reality of the Sasquatch.

Researchers have therefore sought to rely on the physical evidence that does exist. There is certainly plenty of that to be found.

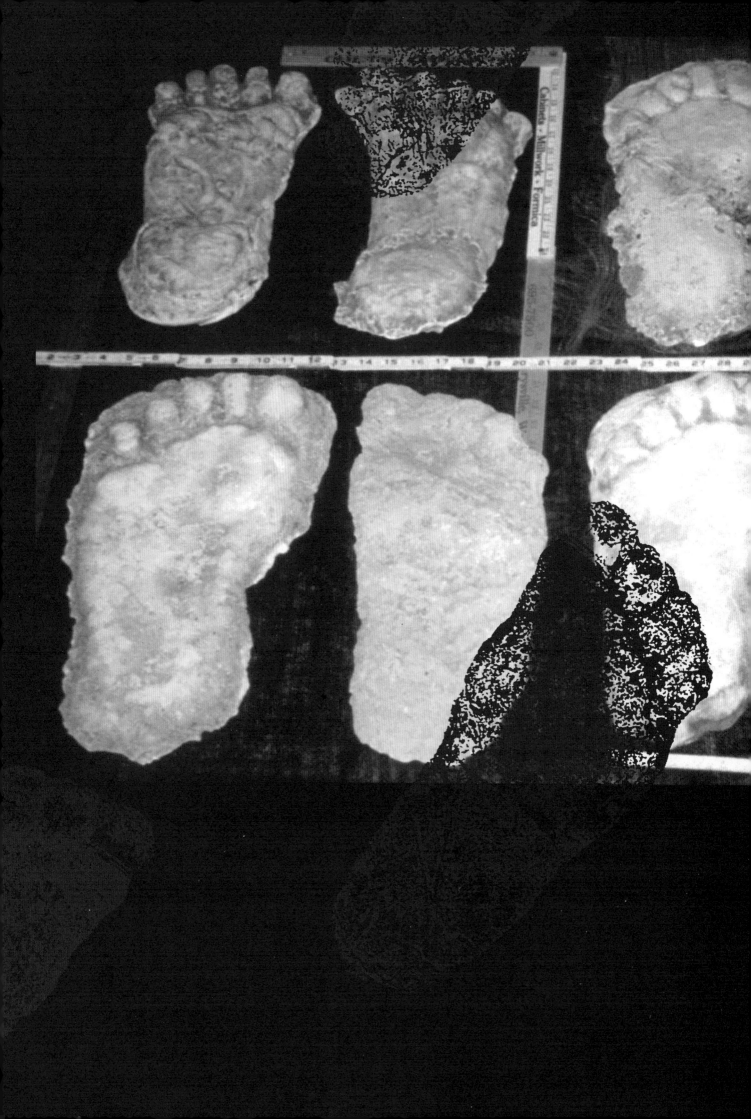

4 Sifting the Evidence

Missing Remains?

All sceptics and scientists are united on one point. They would be convinced that the Sasquatch actually exists if they saw a dead body – or at least a significant part of one such as a skull or several bones. Before moving on to look at the evidence that does exist, it would be worth spending a bit of time looking at the evidence that does not exist. Why is there no Sasquatch body?

One problem that all researchers have to face is that no Sasquatch bodies have ever been found. It could be said that this is because there is no such thing as a Sasquatch. But that would be false logic. There are other possible explanations as well.

If we assume that the Sasquatch exists as a real animal then we must also agree that individuals must die from time to time and leave their bodies. However, we know that the Sasquatch is a relatively intelligent creature – it certainly has the edge in brain power over other large examples of North American wildlife such as cougar or bear. It may even prove to be more intelligent than the gorilla and other large apes. Some researchers believe that it is. It is not impossible, therefore, that the Sasquatch do not much care for the thought of the dead body of a family member being devoured by wolves or cougar and so take steps to hide it from such scavengers. Perhaps they bury the body, perhaps they hide it. Either way the body would not only be hidden from wolves but also from humans.

> One problem that all researchers have to face is that no Sasquatch bodies have ever been found.

If this sounds a bit far-fetched, it is worth bearing in mind that archaeological evidence shows that respect for the dead began very early in human evolution. Neanderthal people certainly buried their dead and there is some evidence that burials might also have taken place among the much more primitive Homo erectus species. An alternative explanation is that the Sasquatch might seek shelter when it felt ill. Thus, a sick or injured Sasquatch would crawl off into a dense patch of undergrowth to be safe from cougar or wolves. If that Sasquatch were to die rather than recover, its body would be left lying where humans would be unlikely to find it.

A third explanation looks to the wolves, cougars, bears and other carnivores that share the range of the Sasquatch. When a creature as big as a Sasquatch dies, the suddenly available meat would make a tasty and nutritious meal for a good number of creatures. Given that these predators are known to take carrion and have an exceptionally fine sense of smell, they could be relied upon to find a Sasquatch body that was left lying about in the open. Within a matter of a few days, perhaps even a few hours, the carcass would be picked clean. For precisely this reason, professional hunters who spend a lot of time out in wilderness areas very rarely come across the dead body of a bear, an elk or a deer.

The scavengers would, however, leave at least some bones behind. These would be scattered over a wide area, but skulls and thigh bones in particular might be expected to survive the attentions of wolves and then lie around in a conspicuous position for a passing human to spot. In other places and habitats this is undoubtedly the case, but not in the mountainous forests of the Pacific seaboard. These forests have a naturally very acidic soil which is usually overlaid with equally acidic coniferous leaf litter and assorted debris. Bones are highly susceptible to the leaching effects of acid. Any bone left lying on the surface of the ground would within a few days suffer from a loss of calcium and other minerals. It would become liable to fracture if touched by a passing animal and could crumble away to dust in a surprisingly short time.

In conclusion, it is hardly surprising that no Sasquatch body has been found. What is more surprising is that anybody could think that one might be.

Pulling the trigger

But if no Sasquatch that has died from natural causes has been found, what about the possibility that a Sasquatch might be shot by a hunter? This has not yet happened. In part this is because relatively few people who have encountered a Sasquatch had a gun on them at the time. Out of those that carried a gun, few saw the creature long enough to get a clear shot. Some people have been in a position to shoot a Sasquatch, but a high proportion say that they deliberately chose not to do so because they felt that shooting one would be more akin to murder than hunting.

In a very small number of reports a person has shot at a Sasquatch in conditions where a hit was likely. And yet there is still no body. If the Sasquatch that was shot at was a real animal, this requires some explanation. Experiences with bears of a similar bulk to that claimed for a Sasquatch would indicate that even a mortally wounded animal can cover a fair distance between being shot and actually dying. Sasquatch that have been shot at have been reported to cry out and then run off. That would be perfectly natural, as would the human's decision not to follow a large, wounded and potentially very aggressive animal into thick cover.

There are also instances where the reaction of a Sasquatch to being shot was entirely unnatural. On the evening of 6 February 1974, a lady living in a rural house near Uniontown, Pennsylvania, heard her dogs barking as if an intruder was approaching. She looked outside to see a hairy, human-like figure in her yard, which seemed to be about 7 feet (213 cm) tall. She picked up a shotgun, opened her door and stepped out on to the porch to get a better look. When she switched on the yard light, the figure turned towards her, raised its arms over its head and started walking towards her. Thinking she was about to be attacked, the woman lifted her shotgun and blasted the creature at point-blank range. There was a sudden flash of light and a loud bang, whereupon the creature vanished into thin air.

Fossilized hominid footprints in Oregon's Warner Valley: they either belong to early First Nation people or to a very large primate.

Such odd reports would explain why a body is not found, but they would also tend to rule out the Sasquatch as a real creature. We shall be looking for an explanation that draws together all the disparate elements of the Sasquatch enigma in the next chapter. For now it is enough to note that the lack of a body does not necessarily mean the lack of a real creature.

The best examples of evidence for the existence of the Sasquatch are the thousands of footprints that have been found in the forests where it is said to live. Some of these are isolated footprints in patches of mud, but others come from trackways that run over considerable distances.

One track found in August 1967 ran along a dirt road in British Columbia for over half a mile and consisted of about a thousand footprints. Many hundreds of these tracks have been photographed or preserved as plaster casts, so it is possible to use them to determine whether newly found footprints are consistent with Sasquatch sightings.

Before the days of tagging animals with radio collars to record their movements, one of the prime methods used by naturalists to study large mammals in the wild was to use the tracks they left behind. It can be surprisingly difficult to locate a wild mammal if it does not want to be found. In 2004 a professional wildlife camera crew was sent by the BBC into the western Himalayas to film snow leopards. They spent over five months in the mountains, but came back with only about 45 seconds of footage good enough to broadcast. The footprints left behind, however, were much easier to locate and to study.

From studying the footprints of animals it is possible to deduce how many of them are living in a particular area, how large they are and, very often, what sex they are. The habits of the creatures in general can be worked out from the places in which the footprints are found. Individual actions, such as drinking, feeding or sleeping can be seen in the footprints. When dealing with larger mammals, it is possible to work out the habits and accustomed actions of individuals, even to the extent of ascribing individual characters and names to them.

Colonel Jim Corbett was a noted big game hunter before the Second World War. He was frequently sent for by the British authorities in India if a tiger or leopard turned man-eater – such things being more usual when the numbers of those carnivores were much greater than today. He invariably began his hunt by studying the pugmarks of the suspected man-eater, as well as those of any other tigers in the area. Only after having identified the particular man-eater from its pugmarks would he begin the hunt, ignoring the other carnivores of the area. Very often he never saw the man-eater until he came to shoot it, having spent the previous weeks getting to know it from its tracks alone. Many other hunters and naturalists have likewise been able to identify and study animals.

Faking It

It must at first be admitted that some of the Sasquatch footprints that have been reported are probably fakes. Sceptics would hold that all of the prints are hoaxes and even the most dedicated Sasquatch believer will accept that some evidence is fraudulent. Writing in 1989, Grover Krantz estimated that up to half of all the supposed Sasquatch footprints that were reported were either fakes or else they looked like fakes. Except in cases where the fraudsters have confessed or been unmasked it is almost impossible to know which prints are real and which are not.

A knowledge of animal behaviour can, however, be used to dismiss obvious fakes. When a wild animal leaves a track it is not a simple matter of a foot being pushed down into soil, mud or snow to leave a print. The creature that leaves the tracks is moving and the footprints show the traces of this. Toes may dig in to get a grip when going uphill, or splay out on mud. If the creature changes direction, the foot will twist, and so distort the print it leaves behind.

Nor is the foot a solid object. Even the foot of a wild Sasquatch, with pads of hardened skin on the soles of its feet, is a relatively soft object. It will fold around stones and other hard objects so that a footprint may well have a stone sticking up inside it.

Most fakes are made by people using wooden plates carved to the size and shape of a Sasquatch footprint. These are then tied on to the feet and the faker walks around, leaving behind impressive-looking tracks. Such crude fakes are easily identified. The footprints left by the wooden feet show no signs of movement: each print is identical to the last. Moreover, the depth of the footprint will reveal the fact that the creator weighed much the same as a human, whereas the Sasquatch has a far greater weight. Strapping on a heavy backpack will increase the depth of the footprint, but it will make it almost impossible for the faker to move about except on level, firm ground.

The famous hoaxer Ray Wallace used this method of making false Sasquatch tracks. He would strap on his wooden feet and go striding about on and beside trails that he knew to be heavily used by urban vacationers, who would have a limited knowledge of wild animal tracks. His efforts led to a large number of reports being made, and they

Dr Grover Krantz holds up the controversial Bossburg prints which seem to indicate clubfoot deformity.

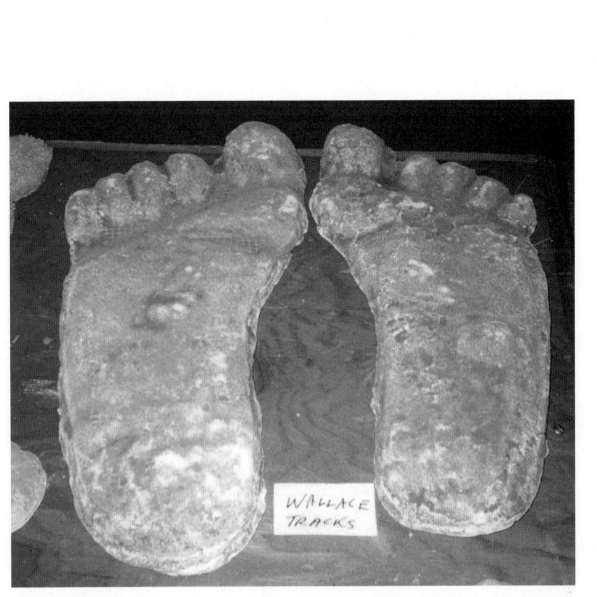

Undoubted fakes: these prints were made by Ray Wallace using a pair of hand-carved wooden feet.

often led to newspaper stories, but they were usually quickly revealed for what they were once a researcher got to see them at first hand.

A more sophisticated method of faking Bigfoot tracks emerged in the later 1980s. A number of tracks and footprints began to be found which, although obviously not created by wooden feet, were suspect. They had been made by a soft foot-like object, but while they showed some signs of dynamic interaction between the foot and the ground they did not show the foot or the toes moving or flexing in any way. Researchers were suspicious, but puzzled. It was Donald Baird, of the Carnegie Museum of Natural History, who worked out how they had probably been produced. Baird was a palaeontologist who specialized in latex and rubber moulds and he brought those skills to bear on the problem.

The starting point is the need for moulds, which can be produced by carving wood to the shape of a pair of Sasquatch feet. These moulds can then be carefully filled with alternating layers of silicone rubber and cheesecloth to give the desired mix of strength and flexibility. Once the compound reaches a thickness of about an inch the work of laying down a false track can begin.

First a site needs to be found where the surface is firmer rather than soft. The person laying the fake trail needs to cover his or her own shoes in bags containing padding so that they will not leave a track. The first print should be made by putting the fake foot on to the ground and then tamping it down by repeatedly hitting a wooden pad inside the foot with a hammer. By using a small pad, different parts of the foot can be struck with different amounts of force, so imitating a living foot that might exert more thrust on the heel than on the midsection. With practice this process can be used to leave a track that gives a more realistic appearance than one made using a cruder method. The soft latex will ensure that stones are left standing proud of the main print, while differential hammering will give an illusion of foot movement.

> The person laying the fake trail needs to cover his or her own shoes in bags containing padding so that they will not leave a track.

Such a method can create surprisingly realistic prints, but even so it cannot mimic a muscled foot that changes its shape or grip during a step, nor is it much good on softer ground. Once researchers knew how the fake could be done, they could spot the frauds more easily.

What seemed to be one such trail was found in January 1991 near Mill Creek, Washington State. It was investigated by Oregon-based researcher James Hewkin. At first sight the actual footprints seemed genuine enough: it was the configuration of the track that raised suspicions. The track began high on a snow-covered hill, ran down through woods to cross a field where winter wheat was starting to sprout, crossed a road, headed for a stream, then cut back to the road where the footprints ended.

The fact that the trail ended at a road was suspicious in itself. Moreover, for much of their length the footprints showed a clear tendency for the feet to be splayed, a human characteristic. Where the tracks crossed a fence, the prints were set exactly where a biped of human height would put them, though the size of the prints indicated that they had been made by a Sasquatch over 7 feet (213 cm) tall. Finally, one footprint was curiously deformed and slashed. Careful analysis showed that the mark had been made by the 'foot' toppling sideways and leaving a flat depression. The conclusion was that the 'feet' were rubber or silicon fakes that had been mounted on flat-sided blocks, probably of wood, and then strapped on to the feet of a human who was about 5 feet 9 inches (175 cm) tall.

The Real Thing?

Frauds apart, there are many thousands of footprints, some of them in clearly defined tracks, that are accepted by researchers as being genuine. It is these that should be studied to see what they reveal about the creature that made them. All that can be done is to concentrate on those that are reported by the more reliable witnesses, who did not seek profit from their findings, and then draw conclusions from the mass of data.

The size and shape of the prints varies greatly. The press gave the Sasquatch the name 'Bigfoot' for the purposes of headline-writing because the footprints discovered by Jerry Crew were so large. Most of the Sasquatch footprints that have been discovered since that time have also been large: lengths of 15 inches (37 cm) and widths of 6 inches (15 cm) are not at all unusual.

But size is not the only distinguishing feature. Sasquatch footprints are a different shape to those of humans and show signs of differences in foot structure as well. The foot of a Sasquatch is wider in proportion to its length than is the human foot. Its heel and toes are more elongated than in a human foot. While the toes are sometimes splayed out, at other times they appear to have been held curved up close to the ball of the foot. The impression received from the prints is that the toes are long and strongly muscled. In addition Sasquatch feet usually leave an impression that is flat across the whole sole because, unlike the human foot, there is no arch. Even a human with fallen arches could not leave a print like that of a Sasquatch.

The human foot (right) lifts off the ground from the ball of the foot; the Sasquatch's flexes in the middle.

There are also clear differences in the way the foot bears the weight of the walker. A human foot carries the weight of the body on the heel as the foot is put down, then on the ball just behind the big toe as the body moves on. The print left by a human walking in a straight line will be deeper at the heel and the ball than elsewhere. As the foot lifts off it will push back at the ball, often scooping a disc of soil out of the print.

Humans have adapted to this method of walking in order to save energy at the expense of grip. Given that humans evolved on the East African plains, the workings of the human foot make perfect sense. Early humans needed to be able to walk considerable distances with relatively little effort while searching for food. The grassy plains provided firm, fairly smooth surfaces on which to walk.

The Sasquatch seem to have adapted to a different sort of walking. Their footprints often show what is known as a midtarsal break. This appears as a clear ridging of the soil or mud about halfway along the foot in a footprint. It is caused by the foot bending at this point as the weight of the animal is transferred to the front of the foot. Human footprints do not show this feature because the human foot simply cannot bend at this point, which is just in front of the ankle: the midtarsal bones are fused solid in a human foot. In some Sasquatch footprints, only the part of the foot in front of the midtarsal break leaves an impression. Again, this is impossible for a human foot.

Built for grip

Another feature of the Sasquatch foot that is seen in the footprints is the long heel. Where the movement of the foot can be deduced from the tracks, it seems that the back end of the heel is some considerable distance behind the shin. This would indicate that the Achilles tendon, which connects the muscles of the shin to the back of the heel, is further back from the hinge of the ankle than it is in humans. The effect of this arrangement would be to increase the leverage exerted by the muscles on the rear part of the foot – exactly what would be needed to apply increased force to a foot that bends halfway along its length.

The stride length of Sasquatch tracks varies widely – presumably due to the speed at which the creature was moving. A creature on a slow stroll will leave footprints closer together than one that is running fast. Where a Sasquatch seems to have been moving in no great hurry, it will typically leave a track with a step length of about 4 feet (122 cm). In addition, each of the footprints is almost behind the other, with all of them pointing in the direction of travel. Again, this is different from a human track where the left and right feet are splayed out on either side of an imaginary line, with the right feet pointing slightly to the right and the left feet slightly to the left.

Putting all of this together gives a fairly clear picture of the type of animal that left the prints. Clearly the creature is bipedal because the marks of its hands or front feet are reported only when the creature was scrambling up or down a steep slope. Not only that but the flexing of the foot would give the walker an increased ability to grip the ground. In humans, the stiff foot makes the toes the key feature of the push-off part of a stride. Having a flexible foot, as indicated by the Sasquatch footprints, transfers the push-off pressure to the front half of the foot and the shin muscles. The toes are thus able to splay out or curl up depending on the surface being negotiated.

Such a flexible foot also increases the area in contact with the ground at each stage of the step. This would tend to even out the depth of the footprint, a feature that characterizes Sasquatch tracks. It also gives a lower pressure load, important for a beast that may weigh up to a thousand pounds.

A stride of around 4 feet (122 cm), a foot about 16 inches (40 cm) long and a midtarsal break would indicate a height of around 7 feet (213 cm). This is, indeed, the sort of height reported for Sasquatches by witnesses. Moreover, the midtarsal break would give the Sasquatch a gait that is quite different from that of humans. Humans bob up and down as they walk because of their stiff feet, but Sasquatches would not show such an obvious vertical movement as they walk. Again, this is a feature that has been noted by witnesses who have seen a Sasquatch walking.

> Humans bob up and down as they walk but Sasquatches would not show such an obvious vertical movement. Again, this is a feature noted by witnesses who have seen a Sasquatch walking.

Hard surface

Another feature of the Sasquatch stride, as reported by witnesses, is that the knee does not lock so that the leg is straight. This is known as a compliant gait. Humans will sometimes adopt this way of walking for short periods of time, usually as a reaction to a very hard surface or to carrying a heavy weight. Given the great size of the Sasquatch, the habitual use of a compliant gait is probably due to its weight.

All of this evidence suggests that the anatomy of the Sasquatch foot is close to that of the great apes. Gorillas, chimpanzees and other apes use their long toes and the front part of the foot to grip branches as they climb, or to hold food objects as they feed. The big toe sticks out sideways like a thumb to aid this grip function. It would seem that the Sasquatch big toe moved to face forward as it became bipedal, but that the toes and the front of the foot retained the ability to grip. This might be a result of the animal living in a mountainous, forested region. The ground in such areas is often broken and uneven, with frequent bumps and dips. The Sasquatch would need to deal with all of this while remaining able to negotiate steep slopes with ease. The apparent structure of the Sasquatch foot, as revealed in its prints, would be more suited to this purpose than the human foot.

Many researchers have noticed that some Sasquatch tracks seem to have been made by feet identical to those that made other tracks in a similar area. This might indicate that a single creature was making the prints.

This phenomenon is not usually used as evidence that the Sasquatch is a real creature for the simple reason that sceptics can argue that it was not the same Sasquatch but the same hoaxer.

Washed away by rain

But there is one interesting example that relates to the Patterson film. Roger Patterson went back to the area where he shot his film because of reports of new Bigfoot tracks left by a family group. The footprints seemed to be those of one large individual, one that was slightly smaller and a third that was significantly smaller. At the time the tracks were seen as being made by a male, a female and their offspring.

These prints were washed away by rain before Patterson arrived on the scene. He had not been in a position to fake them or even to see them and so produce a false foot based on them.

It was not until some years later that somebody thought to compare the footprints cast at the site of the Patterson film with those that had later been found in the same area. The new casts from the Patterson site turned out to match one of the earlier sets of footprints almost exactly.

This again seemed to indicate that the Patterson film was of a genuine Sasquatch. As Patterson had not seen the earlier footprints it was unlikely that he could have faked footprints to match them.

What was surprising was that it was not the slightly smaller 'female' set that matched, but the larger 'male' set. Given that the creature filmed by Patterson is quite clearly a female, this must mean that the family group was not a mated pair with their offspring but an adult female accompanied by an almost-adult Sasquatch and another that was much younger.

It is not only footprints and tracks that form evidence for the Sasquatch. Other marks left behind by what seem to be Sasquatch have been discovered and analyzed.

All Fingers and Thumbs

In 1962 a passing Sasquatch leant against a house near Fort Bragg, California, and left its hand print behind. The outline of the print was traced by the house owner, who said that no internal features such as knuckle joints could be made out. It was 11 inches long and most of this length was taken up by the wide, flat palm. The fingers were relatively short and stubby, and of almost equal length, while the thumb was nearer to the fingers than the wrist and was likewise rather stubby.

In 1980 Bob Titmus was following a Sasquatch track when he reached a spot where the creature had climbed a steep, muddy bank. On top of the bank was a handprint that lay exactly where a tall human-like creature would have put its hand to help pull itself up. A plaster cast was taken. The key feature of the thumb print is that it is facing in the same direction as the fingers. If you hold out your own hand and look at the digits you will see that your thumb faces in towards the palm while the fingers are all facing downwards. Known as the opposable thumb, this is a distinctive human feature that no

other ape has. The opposable thumb makes possible what is known as the precision grip, used when you hold a pencil or a screwdriver, for instance. It allows a human to manipulate small objects with great dexterity, care and precision.

Without it, a human hand would only be capable of what is termed the power grip, the type of grip used when wielding a hammer or an axe. This is fine for exerting brute force, but it does not allow for either delicacy or precision. It would seem from Titmus' handprint that the Sasquatch cannot manage a precision grip.

In 1986 Paul Freeman found and cast another hand print, this time produced by a Sasquatch that had been apparently crouching down to drink. It confirmed that the thumb was incapable of the precision grip, but it seemed to give the additional information that the index finger was almost incapable of moving independently of the other fingers. This is a feature found in most great apes, such as gorillas and orang-utans, but not in humans.

Paul Freeman in 1994 showing footprints that had recently been cast from the Upper Dry Creek area, Washington.

The Skookum Cast

One of the most impressive tracks left by a Sasquatch, but also one of the most controversial, is the so-called Skookum Cast. As with the Patterson film, the Skookum Cast has come in for a great deal of analysis, not only by those prepared to accept the reality of Sasquatch but also by those who remain sceptical. Again, as with the Patterson film, much of the criticism has come from the fact that the cast was found by people who were expressly going out looking for evidence of Bigfoot activity. Sceptics thought that this made hoaxes or misidentification more likely while others pointed out that only those looking for Bigfoot signs would have noticed the thing in the first place.

The story began in September 2000 when the Bigfoot Field Researchers Organization (BFRO) organised a 10-man expedition into the Cascade Mountains of Washington State. The BFRO is one of the more respected outfits in the business of co-ordinating research into the Bigfoot/Sasquatch enigma. They bring together reports and eyewitness accounts, scientific analysis and discussion groups and their website contains a wealth of information and ongoing blogs. Of relevance to the Skookum Cast episode is the fact that the BFRO organize field trips to the remote regions in which the Sasquatch are said to live. There they carry out a variety of experiments and teach novice researchers the tricks of the trade; showing them what to look for and how to record any finds or sightings.

On this particular trip, the BFRO team explored the wilderness looking for footprints and other signs of Sasquatch. Using loudspeakers, they also played a recording of a call thought to have been made by a Sasquatch, in the hope that it would provoke a response. The team also put out baits of fruit on sites next to soft soil. It was hoped that a Sasquatch might be attracted by the fruit and, in collecting it, leave tracks behind. At first not much happened. A call that might have been a Sasquatch was heard and some large, but poor quality, footprints were seen.

Then, on 22 September, two of the team went out to inspect the fruit baits. One of the baits had been taken. The fruit had been picked up and most of it had been eaten. A few pieces of debris showed the marks of broad, flat teeth. What at first puzzled Derek Randles and Richard Noll was that there were no footprints in the muddy ground where the fruit had been placed. Then they spotted an odd series of marks in the soft soil around the muddy patch. Looking at the marks more closely they thought that some large animal had lain down there. Randles and Noll went off to get LeRoy Fish and other team members.

Returning to the site, they all studied the impression on the soft soil. One of them noticed what seemed to be a heel imprint, another saw what looked like an arm imprint. It was decided to cast the impression in plaster, even though this eventually consumed 200 pounds of the stuff. The final cast measured 5 feet (152 cm) by 3 feet (91 cm) and was carefully shipped out to Seattle where a team of scientists willing to look into Sasquatch evidence was called together. This team included Grover Krantz and Jeff Meldrum, plus wildlife biologist Dr John Bindernagle and African game specialist Dr Ron Brown.

The team carefully cleaned up the cast by removing soil that had stuck to it. Any hair caught in the plaster was bagged up for analysis. That hair would, as expected, turn out to be mostly elk, deer and bear, but there were also numerous strands of hair that could not be identified, but which fitted into the emerging pattern of primate-like features.

The cast itself, once clean, showed that a large creature had lain down and left its body impression. It seemed to be the impression of a large human-shaped creature resting on its left side. The marks of the left forearm, left leg, left buttock and left side of the body were quite clear. The only sign of the right leg was the heel, which had been pushed deep into the soft ground as if to steady the creature. Later on, a closer analysis of the heel imprint showed that it retained the distinct shape of an Achilles tendon and skin ridging, as well as signs that it had been moved at least once. The cast also showed clear marks of hair striations, indicating that the thing that had lain down to create it was covered by thick hair.

The most likely explanation seemed to be that a Sasquatch had seen the fruit, but had decided not to walk into the mud to get it. Instead it had lain down next to the mud and then reached out with its right arm to grab it.

News of the find was announced by way of a press release on 23 October 2000. Because Dr Meldrum had studied the cast the press release went out from the Idaho State University, which meant that it carried much more weight than if it had come from BFRO. The release was suitably cautious, stating only that the cast 'constitutes compelling and significant new evidence' rather than claiming that it had definitely been produced by a Sasquatch.

The press release drew responses from sceptics who claimed that it was most likely caused by an elk lying down. However, the link to Idaho University meant that several

> The cast itself, once clean, showed that a large creature had lain down and left its body impression.

specialists were willing to look at the cast. They generally ruled out elk, deer or any other large creature. By 2006 the only explanations that could satisfactorily account for the Skookum Cast were that either a Sasquatch had created it by lying down to reach the fruit or that a hoaxer had produced it.

Looking for Traces

Dramatic as the Skookum Cast was, it was not the only trace claimed to have been left behind by Sasquatch. One of the most interesting of these was mentioned in passing by William Roe in his account of his encounter with a Sasquatch in 1955. After describing the creature and how it behaved, he went on.

'I wanted to find out if it lived on vegetation entirely or ate meat as well, so I went down and looked for signs. I found it in five different places. And although I examined it thoroughly, could find no hair or shells of bugs or insects. So I believe it was strictly a vegetarian.'

What Roe was talking about was scat or droppings. As he realized, studying droppings can tell you a lot about the creature that made them. It can reveal roughly how big it was and what sorts of food it had been eating. More detailed analysis may turn up internal parasites that are specific to a particular species or group of species. That said, it is also an inexact science. In the absence of any other clues, such as tracks, it is possible to accurately identify droppings only some of the time – and that is for known species. For a cryptid such as the Sasquatch the problem is even more complex.

The key issue is being certain that any droppings that have been collected have come from a Sasquatch. Of course, the best way to identify droppings would be to see the animal make them. A second best way would be to collect droppings from beside a track or resting place. Failing that, more general clues, such as size, composition and shape are considered.

Most of the droppings that have been tentatively identified as coming from a Sasquatch have not been found beside a track, but on hard ground where no tracks or footprints were visible. They were picked up as they did not seem to be from any known animal. This does not necessarily mean that they are from a Sasquatch. They might simply be an atypical bear scat.

A few samples of droppings that seem most unlike those of known North American

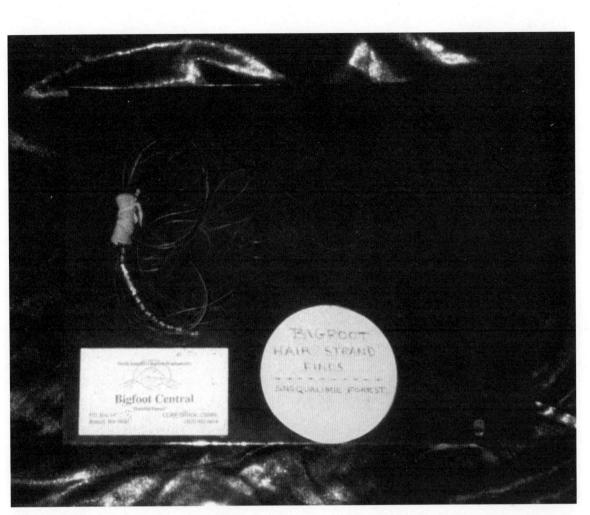

Trace finds include hair found near Bigfoot tracks which could not be attributed to recognized species.

animals have been subjected to various tests. The contents have generally shown that the creature was eating mostly plants – including nuts and seeds – but also some meat. Interestingly one sample contained the eggs of a parasitic worm that lived only in the guts of apes. It could be proved that other samples did not belong to bear, humans, elk or other local animals large enough to deposit such a size of dropping, but it was impossible to be any more definite.

Hairs are another potential source of evidence. Several researchers have collected hairs caught on branches or fences at the site of Sasquatch sightings or beside tracks. Mammal hairs can usually be firmly identified, so long as they are collected in good condition and have not suffered too much from weathering, trampling or other damage. It is sometimes possible to identify the group of animals from which a hair came, even if it is not possible to identify the precise species. The basic problem was stated fairly early on by Ray Pinker, who analyzed hair for the California State College. Asked to analyze some hairs in 1968, Pinker said: 'I could not identify these hairs as Sasquatch until I have a sample of authentic Sasquatch hair to match them to.' He did, however, go on to state unequivocally that the hairs in question did not come from any known North American animal.

Bob Titmus found some hair in 1988 that, when analyzed, was found to be broadly similar to, but distinctly different from, human hair. Hair collected in northern California in 1993 was also unidentified, though it did have some structural similarities to that of a gorilla. Dr Henner Fahrenbach, a biomedical research scientist, has put together a collection of these unidentified hairs. The idea is to try to produce a consistent profile of characteristics that crop up repeatedly. It is hoped that this might eventually produce evidence that some of the unidentified hairs are coming from the same species of animal, thus establishing that there is a species of mammal living in North America that is not yet identified by science. As yet not enough good quality samples have been collected and analyzed, but the work goes on.

Sasquatch 'Nests'

Rather rare discoveries in the forests are what appear to be Sasquatch sleeping nests. When he returned from his claimed kidnapping by a Sasquatch, Albert Ostman mentioned that the creatures had slept on what he called 'blankets' made out of woven fir branches and moss. When recalling the backtracking he had done on the Sasquatch that he had seen, William Roe said: 'I found one place where it had slept for a couple of nights under a tree.' Unfortunately he did not elaborate on what this temporary resting place looked like nor how he recognized it as a sleeping site.

On 13 May 2001 researcher Kathy Moskowitz came across three structures in the forests near Sonora, California, that seemed to have been deliberately constructed. They were each built out of natural materials that could have been gathered nearby. Since Sasquatch had been reported in the vicinity, she suspected that they might be nests or sleeping areas. The largest and most complete of the nests was unusual in that it had a roof formed out of a 12-foot-tall (3.5 m) oak sapling that had been bent over and held down with a large rock. A number of pine branches were then leant against, or pushed into, the branches of the sapling to form a solid wall of vegetation that would have effectively kept out wind or rain. Finally, the sheltered floor of the nest was padded with leaves, ferns, moss and other vegetation.

Other researchers have found similar structures, as well as piles of pine branches or

Twigs and branches found inside an alleged Bigfoot nest were carefully arranged to provide a bed.

ferns, that might be nests. Most of these structures were found in wooded areas and lay on the ground with no attempt at overhead cover.

One apparent nest was found in 1988 inside an abandoned mine entrance. It measured 4 feet (122 cm) by 4 feet 6 inches (137 cm). The base was made of piled sticks that had been covered over with a layer of dead leaves. On top of this was a thick layer of fresh leaves, moss, ferns and other vegetation. It gave the appearance of having been used several times over a long period, with the top layer replenished with every use.

Other than the examples seen by Roe and Ostman, there is no direct evidence that these nests were built or used by Sasquatch. Nobody has seen a Sasquatch sleeping in one, nor have tracks been followed that lead to a nest.

However, the construction of the nests would require hands to manipulate the branches and other components. The only possible candidates for the builders of these nests are Sasquatch or humans. Some eyewitnesses have seen Sasquatch resting, but without any sign of a nest. Usually the creatures have been resting on their sides, but on one occasion the creature was lying on its stomach with its knees pulled up.

Trampled branches seemed to have been pushed flat by a large creature of some kind, very possibly a Sasquatch.

The idea of nests has led to a theory to explain another sign often found in relation to Sasquatch activity: broken saplings and torn branches. It may be that these are signs of anxiety or fear on the part of the Sasquatch. Chimpanzees are known to indulge in this sort of activity when disturbed, though whether it is territorial marking behaviour or a display of strength is not clear.

In 2007, researchers became aware of another type of structure that might be constructed by Sasquatch. As so often in cryptozoology the existence of these 'snow mounds' was fairly well known to locals, but they had not been mentioned to outsiders as none of those who had found them realized their significance.

The snow mounds take the form of a mound of snow about 3 or 4 feet high (91–122 cm) and up to 12 feet (3.5 m) across. Once the mound has been gathered together and its surface smoothed over, it is covered by a thick layer of wood chips, bark, branches and other woody debris. The woody material is usually arranged so that it entirely covers, and so insulates, the snow. When the snow covering the ground melts away the snow mound remains intact, taking several days to melt away. However, when snow mounds have been dug into they have been found to contain nothing but snow.

What these structures are for, and even whether they are related to the Sasquatch enigma, is a hotly debated topic. The sites on which the snow mounds have been found have generally been far from human habitations or, given the deep snows of the high country, human activity at the times they were built. That they contain nothing but snow would seem to rule out the idea that they were constructed to keep some kind of stored food cold. Like so much to do with the Sasquatch, it is a mystery.

Some researchers have recorded what they claim are the calls of Sasquatch. These apparent calls come in a wide variety of whoops, whistles, shrieks, growls and wails. They sound eerie enough even when listened to in the comfort of a civilized home or a studio: out in the woods they must be utterly disturbing.

The idea of nests has led to a theory to explain another sign often found in relation to Sasquatch activity: broken saplings and torn branches. It may be that these are signs of anxiety or fear on the part of the Sasquatch.

Some of these recordings have been subjected to a form of analysis that examines the sound wavelengths and internal structures of the call. These have managed to rule out most of the native North American wildlife as the origin of the sounds. They have not ruled out humans as the source of the sound. This might indicate that the calls are hoaxes, or that the creature making them has a vocal system similar to that of humans.

5 The Real Sasquatch

Real, Living Animal

The recent focus among Sasquatch researchers has been to collect solid evidence to try to prove that the Sasquatch exists as a real, living animal – or at least to prove that the subject is worthy of investigation by a body with the resources and cash to mount a serious and far-ranging expedition. Footprint casts, droppings, recordings of calls, photographs of nests and much more have been collected, and there have been a few videos and photographs of Sasquatch as well.

In all this hive of activity and the press coverage that it generates, it is easy to forget that eyewitness accounts still make up the bulk of Sasquatch reports. Although some people believe that a single species of upright-walking ape is responsible for all the related reports and evidence, it is also easy to overlook the fact that this theory is still very much unproven. It is nothing more than an idea. Proving it would be a simple matter, though – all that is needed is for somebody to capture a Sasquatch or bring in a body or some bones. That nobody has yet done this does not prove that the Sasquatch does not exist, only that it is highly elusive.

However, the Sasquatch theory is proving to be relatively, though only relatively, easy to sell to the scientific establishment. Back in 1967, when Roger Patterson showed his film of a Sasquatch to a panel of scientists in New York it was dismissed out of hand. The reasoning of the scientists then could be summarized like this: 'We know that no wild ape lives in America, so this film must be a fake.' Since then the mass of evidence that has been produced has caused a number of scientists to change their minds. These days the reaction is more likely to be 'Sasquatch is an interesting idea, but I would like to see more evidence before I get involved.' That is progress!

However, not all the evidence that has been collected actually supports this theory. It is by no means certain that there is just one species of unknown ape in North America, nor that there are any apes living wild there at all. The explanation for all the evidence may be more complex, or more simple, than the Sasquatch researchers who support the idea of a single unrecognized species are willing to accept.

The Skunk Ape

A series of reports from the southeastern area of the United States have attracted much less publicity and interest than those from the northwestern states. They are, however, just as internally consistent and appear to be no less credible. Some

The Myakka Ape photos purport to show a Florida Skunk Ape, a creature like an orang-utan. See p.109.

researchers treat these reports as if they were part of the same Sasquatch enigma. Others tend to ignore them because they do not fit the pattern for the Sasquatch of the forested mountains of the west. Some, however, see them as evidence of something different from the Sasquatch. Locally, the sightings and evidence are attributed to a creature called the Skunk Ape, a name given to it because of the terrible smell that is so often reported. Florida is the site of the majority of the reports, so the creature is sometimes called the Florida Ape.

Four teenagers parked up on a quiet rural road in January 1967 were startled when something big and heavy suddenly landed on top of their car.

The earliest report that contains what were to become the traditional features of the Skunk Ape was made in 1900. The local newspaper in Hannibal, Missouri, reported that a strange ape creature had been seen on an island in the Mississippi. It had been captured by a passing circus, which claimed that it was their escaped orang-utan. They had not, however, reported a missing animal, and orang-utans cannot swim, which makes it something of a puzzle as to how the creature got to the island. A second report comes from 1949. Two fishermen out on Sugar Creek, Indiana, were chased off by a rather aggressive creature that they identified as a 'gorilla'. However, it was not until the 1960s that reports began to be made in any real numbers.

Something moving in the trees

In 1966 Mrs Eula Lewis, who lived near Brooksville, Florida, reported that she had been chased into her house by an ape-like creature with a round head and long arms. In July of the same year Ralph Chambers spotted what he called a hairy man moving through forests bordering the Anclote River in Florida. He said it 'had a rancid or putrid odour'. On the evening of 30 November that same year a lady, who preferred to remain anonymous in the newspaper accounts of her experience, got a puncture when driving along a rural road near Brooksville, Florida. She got out to change the wheel and was halfway through the process when she saw something moving in the trees. Worried that it might be somebody up to no good, she looked more closely and saw an ape-like figure covered in hair. As it got closer, the figure's eyes seemed to glow a weird greenish colour as they reflected the light from her torch. She got back into her car and waited for a passing vehicle that she could flag down.

Four teenagers parked up on a quiet rural road in January 1967 were startled when something big and heavy suddenly landed on top of their car. The thing then bounced down on to the bonnet and peered in before bounding off. They described it as a hairy ape-man and reported that it had smelt absolutely awful. In July 1968 near Kinlock, Missouri, a 'gorilla' suddenly appeared in a backyard of a rural house. The creature grabbed hold of a small boy, but dropped him and bounded off when an adult intervened.

Charles Robertson was walking through a guava orchard near Davie, Florida, in 1969 when he was confronted by a hairy 'man-monkey thing' which growled at him. Robertson prudently backed off. A rather less aggressive Skunk Ape was that encountered by H. Osbun and a friend when they were camping out in the Big Cypress Swamp area of Florida. At around 3am Osbun woke up to hear what he took to be some sort of animal snuffling about outside the tent. Thinking that it was a raccoon or something similar after their food, Osbun threw open the tent flap and shouted. He was alarmed to find himself looking at a chimpanzee-type creature the emitted a horrible stench. The animal glanced round at Osbun then fled into the night.

Then in August 1971 a Broward County rabies control officer named Henry Ring was sent to investigate reports of a wild ape that was causing a nuisance to homeowners in a rural area of the county. He found no apes, but he did notice some strange tracks that looked as if a man had been walking about on his hands and knuckles. These are exactly the sort of tracks that would be left by a large ape. Most apes support their weight on four limbs, with the hands of the front limbs curled into a fist and the weight put on to the knuckles.

A pair of workmen had a strange experience in May 1973. They were working on some holiday houses in the Everglades, near Naples, when on the second day, just as dusk was drawing in, one of the men heard something moving about in the swampy forest nearby. He looked up to see a pair of eyes glaring at him from the undergrowth, about 20 feet (6 m) away.

> The creature came out of the trees with an odd waddling gait. Then it grabbed some of the food that they had been preparing to cook on a camp fire...

At first he thought it was a bear, but when it moved he saw that the face was more like that of a human. Around it were strands of long, wispy hair. The man was concerned for his safety so he began to back off. When he felt that it was safe to do so he ran to a house where the men had some guns.

The men watched from the windows as the creature came out of the trees. It walked on its hind legs, but with an odd waddling gait. Then it grabbed some of the food that they had been preparing to cook on a camp fire before slipping back into cover. With hindsight the main witness thought that the closest thing to what he had seen was an

Jennifer Ward had an encounter with a 'Skunk Ape' in August 2004 on a remote Florida road.

orang-utan. When the men emerged from the house, they noticed a strong smell that one of them thought was like that of a pigsty that needed a good clean.

In August 1979 another team of workmen was sent to demolish a remote farmstead near Ochopee in Collier County, Florida. After they had looked around, some of the men climbed up on to the roof to begin work. They noticed a foul smell coming from the cellar, but assumed that some dead animal was inside and so did not investigate.

When they had been working for a couple of hours one of the men on the ground gave a yell. He had seen a creature climb out of the cellar. His shout brought all the men to his side. They saw the animal walk upright across the open ground to some trees about 40 yards distant.
There it turned to sit down and look at the workmen. The beast was about 5 feet (152 cm) tall and was covered all over in long reddish-coloured hair. After several minutes it stood up again and plunged into the dense forest. The curious workmen then investigated the cellar and found a pile of sacking and rags that appeared to have been the creature's sleeping area.

A photo allegedly showing a Skunk Ape of Florida, though its features are different from those in many other reports.

Sightings from cars have been common. For instance, a woman was driving back to her rural home in December 1985, after completing her night shift at work. Motoring along the highway from Tavares she saw a large animal move out of the woods. The creature was walking on its hind legs only, but she did not get a very good look at it. She slowed down as she passed the place where it had entered the trees and wound down the car window to get a better look. Although she could not see anything she was hit by a deeply offensive stench.

Another road-related sighting came in August 2004 when Jennifer Ward was driving through Polk County, Florida. It was evening and her two young daughters were asleep in the back of her vehicle. As she passed near Green Swamp she saw what she took to be a human bending down in a roadside ditch. She slowed down to find out if she could offer any help. As she was about to get out of the car, the figure stood up. Ward was shocked to find herself confronted by a hairy, ape-like figure about 8 feet tall. Putting the safety of her daughters ahead of any curiosity, Ward drove off at speed.

Close to Green Cove Spring, Florida, in 1986, a mother and her son had a similar experience when they were driving along State Route 209 late one evening. Suddenly a human-like figure, about 5 feet (152 cm) tall and covered all over in hair, appeared in the headlights. It glanced quickly at the approaching vehicle and then bounded off the road to slip away among the trees.

In 1993 some interesting tracks were found in the swamps of Collier County. A hunter was out looking for hogs when he found the tracks of two creatures walking in a bipedal fashion. One of the creatures was obviously much larger than the other, which might have been a juvenile. The footprints were shaped like a human hand, but one that was slightly deformed and the larger creature had a stride of almost 6 feet (182 cm). Because the tracks were quite unlike any the man had ever seen in Florida before

Over many decades, Bigfoot researcher Loren Coleman has amassed some of the best evidence on record.

he referred to a text book when he got home. He found that the closest match was the hind foot of a gorilla.

Another road encounter took place on Turner Road outside Everglades City in 2001. This time the creature was squatting by the side of the road. It was about 3 feet (91 cm) tall when it was in a sitting position. The driver slowed down to get a closer look but as the car approached the animal got up on to all fours. Its front legs were much longer than its back legs and it was covered in brown hair. It then moved off quickly and disappeared into some trees. The driver thought that it looked like a chimpanzee rather than anything else.

When these and other reports are added to footprint casts and other evidence, what seems to emerge is that the Skunk Ape is quite a different creature from the Sasquatch of the northwest. The Sasquatch is routinely described as being a massive creature walking upright like a human. In comparison, the Skunk Ape is usually reported as being much smaller and it either walks on all fours or with a waddling gait if upright. It is generally described as being very like a chimpanzee or an orang-utan. The few footprint casts that have been taken would seem to confirm this because they suggest a foot that is very much like that of an ape. Because the big toe sticks out sideways, perhaps as a tree-climbing aid, the creature's footprints look rather like a human hand.

Most Skunk Ape reports come from Florida, but the creature has also been seen in and around swampy forests throughout the hot southern states. This habitat is very different from the mountainous woods of the northwest, so it would be surprising if the Sasquatch could thrive in both places. Indeed, an orang-utan or chimpanzee-type creature would be more suited to the hot swamp forests than a Sasquatch.

On 29 December 2000 the Sheriff's Office in Sarasota, Florida received a letter addressed to the 'Animal Services Department'. The Sheriff had no such department, so the letter was passed on to the general enquiry desk. When it was opened the envelope contained a long letter and two photographs. The letter was from a lady asking if any local zoo or circus had lost an orang-utan, since one had been visiting her property recently. The two photographs were of the ape and they had been enclosed in order that the animal might be recognized. The Sheriff knew of no exotic animals that had been reported lost but on 3 January he contacted David Barkasy of the nearby Silver City Serpentarium for advice. Barkasy knew all about the Skunk Ape and wondered if the photographs of 'an escaped orang-utan' were actually of the Skunk Ape.

> Most Skunk Ape reports come from Florida, but the creature has also been seen in and around swampy forests throughout the hot southern states.

Unfortunately the letter was anonymous: all the writer said was that she and her husband were retired and were living near the Myakka State Park. In February the pictures and some comments from the letter were released to the local press and media in the hope that the writer of the letter could be persuaded to come forward. To date she has not done so. This, of course, raises the possibility that the Myakka Ape Photos, as they have become known, are a hoax, though it may simply be that the retired lady has no wish to get mixed up in the Skunk Ape controversy.

The photographs were sent to Loren Coleman, a noted Bigfoot researcher, who analyzed them himself before sending copies to assorted photographic and primate experts. All came to the conclusion that the photographs had not been produced by digital tampering or other fraudulent means. The creature that was depicted seems to be very similar to an orang-utan. Even its facial expression is similar to that of an orang-utan that is showing fear or surprise, which would be natural if its evening foraging were suddenly interrupted by a camera flash.

Aberrant Behaviour

It is not just in the southeast of the United States that the evidence points to something different from the classical Sasquatch. Across much of America there are reports of Sasquatch-type creatures that behave in remarkably un-Sasquatch ways. Some of the reports from the 1960s hinted at this sort of aberrant behaviour, which puzzled researchers. The trend really got going, however, in the 1970s.

Among the more famous of these reports was a string of cases from around Fouke in Kentucky. They told of a Bigfoot-type creature that behaved in an aggressive and often terrifying way towards humans. The Ford case was typical.

On the night of 1 May 1971 Mrs Ford was woken up as her bedroom window was pushed open. Through the open window came a hairy arm bearing a large, clawed hand that grasped out for her. Behind the window, Mrs Ford glimpsed an ape-like face. When she screamed the arm and the face retreated. Mr Ford grabbed a gun and ran out of the house just in time to see a Sasquatch figure. He fired, but the creature took no notice and slipped off into the trees. An hour later the beast was back, on this occasion trying to kick the front door down. Ford shot at it again and this time it left for good.

The Fouke cases were made into a low-budget horror movie called *Legend of Boggy Creek*. The film was so successful that it spawned three sequels. The Bigfoot in the movies was even more aggressive than the real-life reports from around Fouke would suggest. It was also successfully violent, while the aggressive creatures encountered by real people were usually strangely unable to do any real damage despite their enormous size, great strength and obvious evil intent.

Joan Mills and Mary Ryan stopped for a picnic near the town of Louisiana, Missouri in July 1971. They had just laid out their meal when a Bigfoot came lumbering out of some nearby bushes. It was making a weird gurgling noise and was behaving in a threatening manner. The two women fled for their car and locked themselves in, but they could not drive off because they had left the keys with their picnic. Then the approaching Bigfoot lumbered up to the car and tried to open the doors. Unable to do so, it turned to the picnic and ate some food before returning to the undergrowth from which it had emerged. Once it was gone Mills retrieved the keys and they drove off.

In the same month, a Bigfoot went to a farm near Shapsville, Indiana, on five separate occasions. Each time it came at night and once it attacked the farm dog, though without inflicting any serious injury. The farmer shot at it several times, but never seemed to be able to hit the thing.

A couple of years later, in June 1973, four teenage girls were in a car sheltering from a thunderstorm when they were approached by an 8-foot-tall (244 cm) Bigfoot that growled and screamed at them. The beast had large eyes that glowed bright red. Although the teenagers drove off at speed the Bigfoot seemed to be able to move even quicker, because they saw it standing beside the road ahead of them as they sped off. When they reached the home of one of the girls the Bigfoot was waiting. After glaring at them with its red eyes, it walked off.

The UFOs Land

Later that year, on 25 October, a 22-year-old farmer's son named Stephen saw a large, red glowing ball fall from the sky and land in a field. Stephen took up a shotgun and went to investigate, accompanied by his 10-year-old brother and a visiting friend. As they entered the field, the three saw that the red ball was floating a few feet above the ground. Beside the ball were standing two large human-like figures with ape-like heads. They were covered with dark hair.

When the Bigfoot figures caught sight of the humans they abandoned the glowing ball and began advancing on the boys. Stephen fired over their heads, but they kept on advancing. He then aimed straight at the lead Bigfoot and blasted it three times at close range. The Bigfoot came to a halt and raised its arm, but otherwise showed no sign of having been hit by the shotgun blast. At this point the red ball rose up and flew off. The creatures watched it and then turned and walked off into a nearby wood.

That same month Jeff Martin had an encounter which involved both a Bigfoot and a UFO on the outskirts of Galveston, Indiana. He was out fishing when he saw a 9-foot-tall (274 cm), pale-coloured Bigfoot about 200 feet (61 m) away. When it saw him, the Bigfoot fled, but Martin gave chase. The creature ran across a road, leapt a wide ditch and disappeared into woodland. Almost instantly a bronze-coloured UFO rose out of the woods and flew off.

When the Bigfoot figures caught sight of the humans they abandoned the glowing ball and began advancing on the boys.

In February of the following year another man in Pennsylvania saw a strange red UFO hovering over woods near his home. When he went out on to his porch to get a better look he saw four or more Bigfoot-like creatures moving around the edge of the wood. He grabbed a shotgun, but both the creatures and the UFO disappeared without approaching him.

The Paranormal

UFOs apart, the Bigfoots being seen in Pennsylvania could behave very strangely. A man was walking his dog in a rural area near Uniontown in November 1973 when he saw a tall, hairy Bigfoot with glowing red eyes standing on the path ahead of him. The area was plagued by wild dogs, so the man had a revolver in his pocket. When the Bigfoot began running towards him with its arms uplifted in threatening fashion, the man pulled out his gun. As the creature got to within 15 feet (4.5 m) of him he fired, pumping six bullets into the thing. The Bigfoot then faded away in front of his eyes.

Reports from other states also show the Bigfoot in a sinister light. At Carlisle, Ohio, in October 1972, a Bigfoot with glowing orange eyes ran across a field, hissing and snarling at the hapless human who saw it. Outside Duluth, Minnesota, an 8-foot-tall (244 cm) white furry Bigfoot walked through a building site, stopping to look inside an unfinished house. Then in August 1976 a Bigfoot was seen near Whitehall, New York State. It had red eyes and was covered in very long hair. Less than a year afterwards, in May 1977, a Bigfoot visited a farm near Wantage in New Jersey. The farmer, Mr Sites, grabbed his .22 Magnum rifle and shot it, but without any effect. He then tried a shotgun loaded with deer pellets, but that had no effect either. The Bigfoot just growled in response, then walked off.

It is hardly surprising that these odd and very untypical sightings tend to be ignored by Sasquatch investigators. Most of those that do pay any attention to the Bigfoot sightings that take place outside the northwest area of North America tend to pay them only cursory attention and try to avoid referring to the ability of these creatures to vanish into thin air, to survive being shot at point-blank range or to hop on board UFOs.

The Eastern Bigfoot

A few researchers, however, have suggested that there might be a subspecies or variant of the Sasquatch. This modified creature has usually gone by the name of the Eastern Bigfoot. It is suggested that this Eastern Bigfoot has developed a more aggressive streak and more threatening behaviour because it lives in closer proximity to humans. If so, the Eastern Bigfoot would be an unusual creature. The usual reaction of large mammals faced by a growing human population is to move away or to become more retiring and nocturnal than they are usually.

It was Jack Lapseritis who put forward a radical idea to explain the curious traits and behaviours of the Eastern Bigfoot. He pointed out that the areas in which these encounters took place were rural regions of states with relatively dense human populations. These were areas from which bear, cougar and wolves had long since been displaced. It was unlikely that Sasquatch populations would continue to live in a place from which other large mammals had fled. He also noted that the actions of some Eastern Bigfoots were not only odd for a wild ape, they were utterly impossible or fantastical. Animals cannot simply vanish into thin air.

Lapseritis suggested that these were not encounters with a real animal at all, but with the paranormal. For this he came in for a lot of criticism and became unpopular with many Sasquatch researchers. They felt that his ideas were undermining their task of trying to convince mainstream science that the Sasquatch was a real animal species.

On 24 June 1989 the Department of Anthropology at Washington State University hosted a Sasquatch (Bigfoot) Symposium in partnership with the International Society of Cryptozoology. In an effort to deliver the broadest possible range of opinion the organizers invited Lapseritis to speak.

The opening of Lapseritis' speech was interrupted by a loud protest which was led by René Dahinden, who objected to his presence.

One of Lapseritis' books had these remarks on the back cover: 'In 1979, Mr. Lapseritis was first telepathically contacted by a Sasquatch and ET simultaneously, which was the shock of his life. To further complicate matters, the contact changed him and he developed psychic ability overnight, which triggered a spiritual transformation.'

The so-called Jacobs Photos were taken in Pennsylvania in 2007 by a camera set up to capture a family of bears. But is the creature shown a skinny Sasquatch or a mangy bear?

Jack Lapseritis has since dropped out of the Sasquatch scene, but his ideas have continued to circulate. They are not as far-fetched as some researchers might think. The paranormal is, by its very nature, unexplained. It is open to widely varying interpretations and conclusions, even among those who profess to believe that it has an objective reality.

In reference to the Sasquatch, it must be admitted that many of the sightings of the Eastern Bigfoot have more in common with the paranormal than with zoology. The link to UFOs in some sightings is one clue, the ability to ignore being shot is another. There are also more subtle clues to the unworldly nature of the Eastern Bigfoot. Supernatural creatures from many parts of the world are said to have eyes that are abnormally large or glow red, or both. It is also the case that paranormal animals are very often aggressively hostile to humans, but never manage to inflict any actual harm. In all of these ways the more bizarre sightings of the Eastern Bigfoot are closer to the horrific Black Shuck of England or the malevolent Vetala of India than to the Sasquatch.

It is also striking that the Eastern Bigfoot was not reported until the events at the 1958 construction camp in Bluff Creek catapulted the Bigfoot into the national media. The pace of sightings increased after the 1967 Patterson film was widely shown and speeded up again after the horror movie *Legend of Boggy Creek* was released. Encounters with paranormal creatures nearly always fit into a type that is already known to the percipient. That does not necessarily mean that the witness invented the encounter or was hallucinating. Some researchers believe that paranormal entities take a form that the witness expects them to take, by some psychic means. It is clear, however, that those sightings of Bigfoots that behaved in paranormal ways began only after the wider American public became aware of the possible existence of the Bigfoot.

The reports of Eastern Bigfoots behaving in bizarre ways were made in all good faith, but whether the reports should be classified with the Sasquatch or with UFOs and ghosts is a matter of conjecture.

A Description of the Sasquatch

Returning to the Sasquatch on the forested slopes of the Pacific mountains, the evidence is far clearer, much more impressive and more indicative of a real animal. But even if it is accepted that the Sasquatch is a real creature, it then needs to be categorized in some way. From the physical evidence, sightings and other material that has been gathered a tentative description of the Sasquatch and its habits can be produced.

Sasquatches are primates that walk on their hind legs and are covered with hair. An adult is around 7 to 8 feet (213–244 cm) tall and weighs around 650 pounds on average. Also, there is some evidence that males are slightly larger than females.

The hair that covers a Sasquatch is generally black to reddish brown in colour, though it may be lighter in places. A comparison with other primates would indicate that it turns paler with advanced age. It tends to be around 3 to 6 inches (7.5–15 cm) in length, but there are some reports of manes of longer hair around the head and neck. These manes may be confined to males. The skin, when it can be seen, is generally dark, ranging from black to brown.

Heads are generally ape-like, rising to a peak at the back. This suggests the presence of a sagittal crest and enlarged jaw muscles while the size of the head indicates a brain capacity that is marginally larger than that of a gorilla. Faces are large with prominent brow ridges, deep-set eyes and wide cheeks, from which the mouth does not protrude markedly; noses seem to be halfway between those of apes and humans. Ears are generally small and are usually hidden under the hair.

> Sasquatches have arms that are heavily muscled and long, reaching almost to the knees.

The bodies of these creatures are massive and muscular, being almost as thick front to back as they are side to side. Their shoulders are wider in proportion to their height than is usual for a human and that width is maintained right down to the equally wide hips. This gives a huge volume for the lungs and the digestive system. Females have visible breasts.

Sasquatches have arms that are heavily muscled and long, reaching almost to the knees. Their hands are large and wide with stubby fingers and short thumbs that are not opposable to the fingers while the legs are also massive and heavily muscled. The feet are wide and they exhibit a midtarsal break: the ability to flex halfway along their length. Finally, the toes are long and prehensile, giving the ability to grip uneven or wet ground.

The Sasquatch seem to be more active at night, as well as at dusk and dawn, than during the day. It must be assumed, therefore, that their night vision is good compared to that of humans. They also have acute hearing and a good sense of smell.

Sasquatch have been seen eating leaves, berries, roots, birds, fish, rodents and deer, so their feeding habits are very wide-ranging. They will dig in the ground with their hands, turn over rocks and logs to find grubs and rodents and pluck vegetation, but they have never been seen using tools or storing food. Although they are known to stalk and eat larger animals, such as deer, how they kill is unclear because neither their teeth nor their hands seem to be well-suited to the purpose. Perhaps they use rocks as clubs.

The massive bodies and powerful jaw muscles of the Sasquatch could be explained by the fact that their diet is largely vegetarian. Plant food is more difficult to chew and digest than meat so their huge body capacity is perhaps designed to accommodate the large digestive system that such a diet demands. It has been estimated that an adult Sasquatch would need about 5,000 calories each day to maintain an active lifestyle so the range of available food sources needs to be as wide as possible.

> The social life of Sasquatches is unclear. Most are observed alone, but tracks often show two or three moving together and a few witnesses have seen small groups of up to half a dozen apparently living together.

The strength of the Sasquatch is considerable. Like other great apes they have a wide repertoire of threat displays that include shaking undergrowth, pounding on tree trunks and throwing rocks. They will also frequently twist saplings, breaking the trunks in a spiral pattern. This may be a way of marking territory or it might be a method of constructing waymarkers so that other family members can follow their trail.

The social life of Sasquatches is unclear. Most are observed alone, but tracks often show two or three moving together and a few witnesses have seen small groups of up to half a dozen apparently living together. Footprints indicate that a female will often have a very young child with her, aged about four or so, as well as as one that is almost adult. This would indicate that the female breeds every five years or so, although the evidence is admittedly thin. The young of the Sasquatch seem to be born in the spring, but again evidence is scant. Their lifespan is unknown, but comparison with other primates would indicate about 35 years.

It seems that the Sasquatch originally lived in forests across North America. However, since the onset of dense European settlement it has retreated significantly and is now confined to the forested mountains of the northwest of the continent. There might be small populations in other forested areas.

Total numbers are open to speculation – estimates have ranged from 2,000 to 10,000 though many would agree that numbers are falling. The Sasquatch does not seem to migrate nor does it have defined territories. Instead it wanders in a nomadic fashion: an individual will stay in an area for a few days and then move on. Sasquatch are seen less often in winter months, which may indicate that they are less active in the very cold weather, when less food is about. They may build sleeping nests for temporary use out of branches, moss, ferns and other gathered soft vegetation.

There has been a great deal of speculation about where the Sasquatch might be positioned on the evolutionary tree. This has been prompted by the fact that its upright stance makes it look human, while its ape-like head and habits make it seem closer to an ape. The problem is almost impossible to solve and until a body can be subjected to DNA testing it will remain so. However, it is fair to note that recent fossil finds have shown that the human evolutionary tree has been considerably more diverse and complex than was previously thought. It is now certain that our human ancestors achieved upright walking long before the brain began to expand or the hand became a precision instrument, as in modern humans. There is plenty of space on the human family tree for a creature such as the Sasquatch, but at the same time it would not be out of place on the ape branch of the primate family.

What Evidence Is There?

Sceptics, of course, refuse to believe that there is a cryptid ape species in North America. Some are no less dismissive of the evidence than the scientists who saw the Patterson film back in 1967. They would argue that if a giant man-ape were plodding about North America it would have been found by now, thereby sweeping aside all the evidence as worthless and giving it no more thought. In 2006, for instance, John Crane, a zoologist and biologist, was quoted in USA Today as saying: 'There is no such thing as Bigfoot. No data other than material that's clearly been fabricated has ever been presented.'

Not all sceptics are so dismissive nor so willing to ignore the mounting evidence. Some are prepared to look at the material that researchers have amassed, even though they find it lacking in credibility.

The fact that even those who accept the Sasquatch cannot always agree on the importance of particular pieces of evidence does not help win over sceptics. In 2000, for instance, tracks were found in Oregon's Blue Mountains. Grover Krantz declared them to be genuine and said they constituted important new proof of the reality of Sasquatch. On the other hand, the equally experienced researcher René Dahinden, who firmly believes in the Sasquatch, took one look and said: 'Any village idiot can see they are fake.'

The most prolific, and the best recorded, examples of evidence for the Sasquatch are footprint casts. The huge tracks that they are taken from are physical proof that something was moving around. But the problem that needs to be solved is what made the tracks. Undoubtedly some tracks are hoaxes, made by humans. This has tended to reduce the credibility of the tracks that appear to be genuine. Although sceptics would argue that they too are fakes, it is simply the case that nobody has yet worked out how they were made.

> The evidence collected to date points strongly to the fact that there is a real upright-walking ape living wild in North America.

The few films and photographs that do exist are, with the exception of the Patterson film, so blurred or of such poor quality that it is impossible to rule out trickery.

Even the Patterson film has been denounced as a fake. Some claim to be able to see a zipper in one or two frames, though it is by no means clear that this is the case. There are also problems relating to the speed at which the film was shot, but these might yet be resolved. However, the movie footage is so clear that it must be either a real Sasquatch or a man in a suit – just because nobody has yet proved how it was faked does not mean that it has to be genuine.

That is, of course, to ignore the background evidence, such as the tracks followed by Titmus, but sceptics might suggest that Titmus was either in on the prank or willing to support Patterson for his own reasons.

Problems with the evidence

One problem with the sound recordings, hair samples and droppings that have been collected is that the best that can be said about them is that they cannot positively be identified as coming from any known animal. That does not necessarily mean that they come from an unknown animal, only that the diagnostic tests did not produce a clear result. This might be down to something as simple as the contamination of a bear hair sample by sweat from the hand of the person who collected it.

In the final analysis, the evidence collected to date points strongly to the fact that there is a real upright-walking ape living wild in North America. But the evidence does not prove that this is the case.

Sceptics are quite right to point out that it is inherently unlikely that thousands of

7-foot-tall (213 cm) apes are roaming about but that nobody has yet been able to catch or kill one. The forested mountains of the northwestern areas of North America might be remote, but they are not that remote. Gorillas have been proved to exist in jungle areas every bit as remote as the suggested home range of the Sasquatch, so why is getting absolute proof of the Sasquatch proving to be so difficult? It would be thought that, one day, a Sasquatch would be found either dead or alive. Every year that slips by without such proof being found, the sceptics argue, is in itself proof that no such animal exists.

On the other hand, Sasquatch might well be a real species, perhaps more than one. If that is the case then humanity will have been guilty of a horrific ecological crime by not protecting its home range and not providing it with the means it needs to survive.

6 The Yeti

The Abominable Snowman

The Yeti, or Abominable Snowman as the press preferred to call it, hit the news headlines in the year 1951. Mountaineer Eric Shipton came back from an expedition to the Himalayas with some photographs that had been taken in the high Himalayan snows. They were of a series of footprints that ran for hundreds of yards across a snowfield. Although the footprints were roughly human in outline they were enormous. The photographs dominated the British newspapers for days and rapidly spread to other countries.

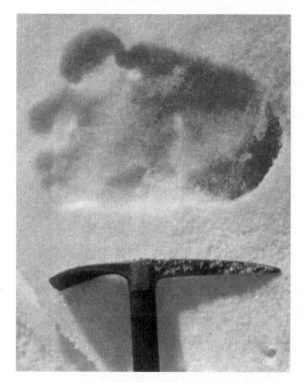

The photo that sparked international interest in the Yeti was taken by mountaineer Eric Shipton in 1951.

Even if the general public was taken by surprise by these dramatic pictures, mountaineers and old India hands were less shocked. For decades they had been hearing stories about the strange half-man, half-ape beasts that lurked in the mountains. The only surprise was that somebody had finally managed to photograph a series of tracks.

The first outsider to hear tales of the strange beasts was the noted hill walker B.H. Hodgson. He was in northern Nepal in 1825 when his porters saw a tall creature covered with long, dark hair, which bounded off in apparent fear. Hodgson did not see the creature himself, but from the descriptions given by his excited porters he thought that it must have been some sort of orang-utan.

In 1889, Major L.A. Waddell was on a mapping expedition in the mountains of Sikkim when he found a trackway of footprints that seemed to be those of a barefooted man with enormous feet. His local guide declared that they belonged to 'the hairy wild man' and insisted that they should leave the area at once.

Another event took place at around this time but it did not become public knowledge until the 1920s, when William Knight wrote to *The Times* about it. Although what he saw was not the Yeti of common imagination it does give a hint of the wide range of experiences that were attributed to the Abominable Snowman. Knight was riding from Tantok to Sedonchen in Sikkim when he stopped to give his horse a rest and sat down beside a track that ran through the heavily forested mountains.

Eric Shipton was an intrepid climber and explorer; he took part in the reconnaissance of Everest in 1951.

'I heard a slight sound and looking round saw, some 20 paces away, a figure which I now suppose must have been one of the hairy men that the Tibetans call the Abominable Snowman. He was a little under 6ft [183 cm] high, almost stark naked in that bitter cold – it was the month of November. He was a kind of pale yellow all over, about the colour of a Chinaman, a shock of matted hair on his head, little hair on his face, highly splayed feet and large, formidable hands. His muscular development in the arms, thighs, legs, back and chest was terrific. He had in his hand what seemed to me to be some form of primitive bow. He did not see me, but stood there and I watched for some five or six minutes. So far as I could make out, he was watching some man or beast far down the hillside. At the end of some five minutes he started off at a run down the hill, and I was impressed with the tremendous speed at which he travelled.'

As the column was about to enter a narrow defile... the rocks echoed to a strange call. Puzzled, Mary MacDonald turned around to ask her guide what animal could make such a noise. She found herself alone. Her guide and porters had thrown down their loads and were running away at high speed back down the track.

It is almost certain that what Knight saw was one of the unfortunate individuals that are driven from their families and villages to live wild and solitary lives in the wilderness. A few of these people are driven out because of crimes they commit, but most are expelled because they suffer from mental health problems. In small, isolated communities there is no real way to care for those who suffer in such ways, so expelling them to live with the wild beasts is not an unusual recourse. Most of these people die, but a few manage to eke out an existence. It would seem that Knight encountered one such.

About ten years later Mary MacDonald, the daughter of a colonial officer, was walking through the mountains close to the border with Tibet. She was on a pleasure ramble lasting a month and had a team of local porters to carry her tent, cooking equipment and supplies. As the column was about to enter a narrow defile on the way to the Garbyang Pass the rocks echoed to a strange call. MacDonald later likened it to the call of a seagull, but very much louder, ending in a throaty roar. Puzzled, MacDonald turned around to ask her guide what animal could make such a noise. She found herself alone. Her guide and porters had thrown down their loads and were running away at high speed back down the track.

Now rather worried, MacDonald retrieved her hunting rifle from one of the abandoned packs, in case the unknown animal turned out to be dangerous, and set off after her porters. She found them grouped on a flat area of ground some two miles from the defile. They told her that the cry had been made by a *metoh kangmi*, or 'bad man of the snow', which was warning them to leave. It was only after much persuasion and some threats that MacDonald got her men to retrieve the abandoned packs, but nothing would persuade them to enter the defile.

Figures on a mountainside

In September 1921 Colonel Howard-Bury was near Lhapka-la on his way to scout out Mount Everest for a climbing expedition. Suddenly his porters started chattering excitedly to each other and then began pointing to the side of a mountain half a mile or so ahead. Howard-Bury looked for the source of their interest and saw three human-like figures walking across a large patch of snow. Some hours later the expedition reached the snowfield and he was able to study the tracks left by the figures. Each footprint was over 14 inches (40 cm) long, but otherwise looked like that of a naked human foot. The porters told Howard-Bury that the figures were not men but *metoh kangmi*.

It was Howard-Bury who translated the phrase *metoh kangmi* as 'Abominable Snowman'. He passed it on to a Calcutta-based journalist named Henry Newman who wrote a few pieces about the mystery animal, again calling it the Abominable Snowman. This was the name that was used when tales of the mystery creature spread through the English-speaking communities of northern India.

Four years later Narik Tombazi, a Fellow of the Royal Geographical Society, also chanced upon an Abominable Snowman. He was studying glaciers in northern Sikkim when he saw a strange figure moving slowly along a path about 2,000 feet below him. The creature was walking upright like a human, but it was covered in dense fur. It stopped every now and then to pluck leaves from bushes and once to uproot a bush and gnaw on its roots. By the later 1920s several Europeans working in the Himalayas had seen unusual footprints and many more had heard tales from the locals about the strange creatures. From the various sources the naturalist Frank Smythe put together a picture of the unknown animal.

The Abominable Snowman was, he thought, an unknown type of ape. The creature stood less than 6 feet (183 cm) tall when upright, but it was much more massive than a human. Its chest in particular was very broad and muscular while its powerful arms hung down almost to its knees. The creature's head had a high-domed skull that Smythe guessed might anchor the strong jaw muscles that would power the teeth when it chewed leaves and twigs. However, its face was rather more human than those of

An artist's impression of a Yeti based on eyewitness reports: it seems more ape-like than the Sasquatch.

Indian monkeys. The animal's legs were slightly bowed and its feet were turned inwards slightly. Its big toe was separated from the others by a distinct gap that showed up in many footprints when it walked upright, as it normally did. When it was in a hurry, though, it would go down on to all fours. In this posture it used the knuckles of its hands to support its weight. The creature was said to live in caves high in the mountains, but it came down to the forested valleys to search for food.

Smythe discounted some of the stories about the creature as mere folklore. For instance, it was said to kill yaks and throw rocks at humans. However, he remained convinced that there was a real creature up in the mountains that was unknown to science. By the later 1930s this view was becoming more widespread in official circles. They had previously ignored the tales as being mere native superstition. But then the Second World War broke out, Japanese armies appeared on the borders of India and everyone had more urgent business to worry about than Abominable Snowmen. Not until Shipton's photographs were taken did the subject again attract attention.

> 'Yeti' is not, in fact, very accurate because it is derived from *yeh-the*, a generic Nepalese term for any large animal that lives in the high mountains.

It was in the postwar period that the name 'Yeti' began to be given to the strange creature. The word is not, in fact, very accurate because it is derived from *yeh-the*, a generic Nepalese term for any large animal that lives in the high mountains. This has led to some confusion over the years. Locals may refer to the Himalayan red bear, which they specifically call the *dzu-the*, as a *yeh-the* since it is large and lives in the high mountains. Those who live in the Himalayas are quite right to be nervous of the red bear. It is notoriously bad-tempered, it will attack without warning and it is strong enough to kill an adult yak with ease. Many later travellers who heard stories about the aggressive Yeti had in fact been listening to tales of encounters with the red bear – the *yeh-the*.

One wartime sighting that emerged only after the Shipton photographs were publicized was that of Slavomir Rawicz. Rawicz was a Polish army officer who had been arrested by the Soviet secret police when the Russians occupied eastern Poland in 1939. He had been shipped off to a Siberian slave labour camp, but had escaped and with a few companions had walked south to cross the Himalayas and reach British India. After the war Rawicz settled in Britain and in 1956 he wrote a book about his wartime experiences. He included a section on the strange experience he had when following a mountain track that crossed from Tibet into Bhutan.

According to Rawicz he saw two figures blocking the path at a range of about 100 yards. At first the refugees took the figures to be bears standing on their hind legs. They expected them to fall down on all fours, but they never did. The creatures did not stop shuffling around on their hind legs. After more than an hour, Rawicz and his companions decided to retrace their steps and find another path. He claims to have been watching the strange creatures all this time.

Rawicz went on to say that the creatures were about 8 feet (244 cm) tall and had squarish heads with no visible ears. The back of their heads was vertical, dropping straight down from the crown and their shoulders sloped down to a powerful chest. Their arms were long and muscular, reaching down to the knees.

Rawicz wrote that the creatures were covered in fur, with what seemed to be a longer coat of hairs over a shorter layer of fur close to the skin. This is an odd description, but if Rawicz is to be believed he watched these two beasts for over an hour at fairly close range so he is unlikely to have got much wrong. As Rawicz himself wrote, 'There was something both of the bear and the ape about their shape.' It is unfortunate that parts of the story told by Rawicz turned out to be untrue, so his account of the two Yetis is usually thought to be unreliable.

The famous Shipton photograph was the result of a November 1951 reconnaissance

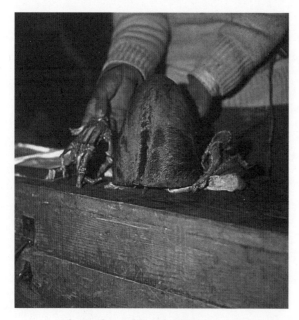

The scalp and hand alleged to come from a Yeti that were kept for many years at the remote Pangboche Monastery.

trip. Its purpose was to discover routes up the lower sections of the Everest massif, in readiness for a later attempt on the peak itself.

Shipton and Michael Ward were exploring the saddle at the top of the Menlung Glacier at around 18,000 feet when they saw a set of tracks left in deep snow.

They followed them for about a mile along the edge of the glacier, but then had to turn back. In order to prove their story they photographed a section of the track and one of the clearest individual prints.

Two years later John (later Lord) Hunt came across another set of tracks which had been left behind in the snow, but unfortunately he did not have a camera with him to record them. At the same time, he also heard the high-pitched yelping cry that is usually credited to the Yeti.

In 1954 the *Daily Mail* financed an expedition to the Himalayas. Their aim was to collect information about the Yeti – and catch one, if possible. The expedition organizers hired 300 porters to carry the equipment up into the high mountains, where hundreds of locals were contacted and vast distances were covered. No Yeti was captured, nor even seen, but the expedition did come back with a wealth of anecdotal evidence and a great boost in sales for the newspaper.

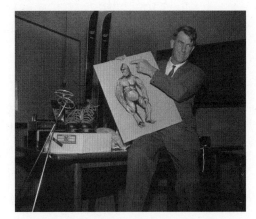

Sir Edmund Hillary shows newsmen a picture of a Yeti: he claimed he would capture one on his next expedition.

Among the more exciting discoveries of the expedition was the fact that two Yeti scalps were kept in Buddhist monasteries at Pangboche and Khumjung. They were used in temple rituals and dances by monks who were pretending to be Yetis. The *Daily Mail* team was allowed to photograph the Pangboche scalp, but they could not borrow it for study. In 1960 the mountaineer Sir Edmund Hillary was allowed to borrow the Khumjung scalp in return for having the monastic school rebuilt. However, the results of the tests he had carried out were disappointing. The skin seemed to have come from the hide of a serow, a form of wild Himalayan goat.

More excitingly, the Pangboche monastery claimed to have a mummified Yeti hand and wrist as well as the scalp. The monastic officials were reluctant to allow Europeans to see the relic, with good reason as it turned out. In 1957 an American team was allowed to see it and another team was given permission to view and photograph it two years later. On this later visit a team member named Peter Byrne reportedly stole a few bones from the wrist and replaced them with human bones. He then wrapped the supposed Yeti hand up so that the replaced bones did not show. Byrne claimed that he handed the bones to the actor James Stewart who smuggled them back to the United States for him. When the bones were later studied they turned out to be almost identical to those of a human, but rather larger and more robust than is normal.

Meanwhile, the Pangboche Hand was studied by Sir Edmund Hillary, who decided that it was a fake made up of animal and human remains mixed together. If Byrne did steal some bones and replace them with human bones this would explain Hillary's findings. In 1992 the hand was stolen from the Pangboche monastery. It has not been seen since and is thought to have vanished into the illegal trade in rare animal artifacts.

The Yeti seems to have had a habit of appearing when it was least expected. This appears to be the case in the following instances.

Don Whillans was camping on an open slope at 13,000 feet in 1970. It was some time after dusk on a sparklingly clear moonlit night and he was resting quietly when he saw something emerge from a patch of nearby woodland. He saw the creature distinctly and he estimated it to be about as tall as a human, but much bulkier. The beast went bounding across the turf on all fours, moving in a similar manner to a chimpanzee.

Only a couple of years later, in 1972, a zoological expedition was camped out in the forested Arun Valley when a large creature came lumbering between the tents after dark. Assuming it to be a bear, the team members stayed in their tents until the creature had gone. When they emerged they found that their visitor had left tracks that looked similar to those of a gorilla.

Then in 1984 mountaineer David Sheppard was near the southern Col of Everest when he saw a large, hairy man-like creature following him for a while.

It seems that the Yeti is still around because Josh Gates, an American television presenter, discovered and filmed a new Yeti track in December 2007. Each of the footprints was about 11 inches (28 cm) long and 8 inches (20 cm) wide.

The sightings by Whillans and Sheppard are the only occasions on which credible European witnesses have seen a Yeti when visibility has been good. There have, however, been numerous sightings by Sherpas and other hill peoples, who spend far more time up in the Himalayas than do Europeans. In the past these accounts have often been dismissed because the Yeti featured in local ritual and religious custom to such an extent that Europeans did not think that a sighting by a local was reliable. More recently the sightings have been treated with a bit more consideration.

For instance, in March 1951 Lakhpa Tensing went up to the hill pastures above Namche to search for a missing yak. He came across a 5-foot-tall (152 cm) Yeti squatting on a rock and eating a mousehare. The Yeti quickly scampered off. A few years later Pasang Nima was leading a caravan over the Nepalese–Tibet border when he saw a Yeti sitting on the grass about 300 yards off the track. The creature was digging in the

Ten Tsing, the Sherpa who climbed Everest with Hillary, was a firm believer in the Yeti.

The 1952 encounter between Anseering and a Yeti on the high Himalayan pastures.

Yak herder Dakhu thought that the Yeti was trying to steal his calf, so he attacked it with his staff.

ground with its fingers, pulling up roots which it then chewed.

The following year, in October, Anseering and his wife went up to the high pastures to look for medicinal roots. They emerged from some trees to see a Yeti apparently picking leaves off a bush. As soon as it became aware of them it bounded off on all four legs at high speed to disappear among a jumble of rocks.

Another villager, Dakhu, met a Yeti in rather different circumstances. He was leading a yak and its calf along a track through the dense valley forests when a Yeti emerged suddenly from the undergrowth. The Yeti approached boldly in what Dakhu took to be an aggressive fashion. Fearing that the beast intended to kill and eat the yak calf, Dakhu flourished his stick at the Yeti. Recoiling from the threat, the Yeti scampered off into the trees and was seen no more.

Meanwhile, a few reports about a creature very similar to the Yeti began to filter out of China. It was said to live on the Chinese side of the Himalayas in Yunan province. The first of these to make an impact appeared in the *Sunday Telegraph* on 22 April 1979 with the heading 'Soldiers ate a Yeti'. Lifted from a Chinese zoological magazine, the story was a third-hand retelling of a news item from 1962. Apparently, soldiers patrolling the passes between China and Tibet got hungry and shot a creature that, from the description they later gave of it, was some large type of ape. They ate the flesh and threw away the bones so there was no solid evidence to back up the story.

Another report came from 1976 and told of how six forestry workers came across a strange tailless animal covered in red-brown fur. The description seemed to be that of an ape. This report prompted the Chinese Academy of Sciences to send an investigation team to look into the matter. They produced a number of eyewitness reports, plus a few strands of hair collected from the bark of a tree against which one of the mystery animals had been seen to lean. The hairs could not be identified.

One of the clearest accounts recorded by the expedition came from Pang Gensheng, a 33-year-old farmer from Cuifeng. This was his story.

'In the summer of 1977 I went to Dadi Valley to cut logs. Between 11 am and noon I ran into a "hairy man" in the woods. It came closer and I got scared so I retreated until my back was against a stone cliff and I could not go any further. The creature came up to about 5 feet [152 cm] from me. I raised my axe, ready to fight for my life. We stood like that, neither of us moving for a long time. Then I groped for a stone and threw it at him. It hit his chest. He uttered several howls and rubbed the spot with his left hand. Then he turned left and leaned against a tree, then walked away slowly toward the bottom of the valley. He kept making a mumbling sound. He was about 7 feet [213 cm] tall with shoulders wider than a man's,

This upland valley used for pasturing livestock in summer was said to be a haunt of the Yeti too.

a sloping forehead, deep-set eyes and a bulbous nose with slightly upturned nostrils. He had sunken cheeks, ears like a man's but bigger and round eyes also bigger than a man's. His jaw jutted out and he had protruding lips. His front teeth were as wide as a horse's. His eyes were black. His hair was dark brown and more than a foot long and it hung loose and long over his shoulders. His face, except for his nose and ears, was covered with short hairs. His arms hung down to below his knees. He had big hands about half a foot long with thumbs only slightly separated from the fingers. He did not have a tail. The hair on his body was short. He had thick thighs, shorter than the lower part of his leg. He walked upright, but with his feet apart. His feet were each about a foot long and half that broad – wider at the front and narrow behind. The toes were splayed out. He was a male – I could see that clearly.'

The picture that emerges from these assorted sightings and other reports is that the Yeti is an ape-like creature that is about 5 feet (152 cm) tall if it stands on its hind feet. It moves habitually on all fours, but it can walk upright for a short distance. The creature seems to be mostly nocturnal, although it will occasionally come out in daylight. It seems to be omnivorous, feeding on plants and on small animals when it can catch them. Most sightings of the Yeti or its footprints are of a solitary animal. It has been speculated that these may be young males driven out of the family group to find a new territory, which would explain why they are seen at all. A creature in unfamiliar territory is more likely to be spotted than one on its home ground. It also seems to be the case that the usual home of these creatures is not on the high, snowy mountains, but in the densely forested valleys. This would make sense because that is where it would be most likely to find food.

However, the existence of an unknown ape species is not the only explanation for the evidence. It is well known that when exposed to bright sunlight, crisp snow can evaporate straight to water vapour without first forming meltwater. When this happens, any marks in the snow can become enlarged, sometimes quite spectacularly, without there being any obvious signs of melting. It is possible that some of the huge footprints that have been discovered on the high snows have been enlarged in this way.

The back of beyond

The prime suspects for leaving such tracks are the *sadhus*, or holy men, who make a habit of living in the most remote places and in conditions of the utmost privation. Their aim is to be free of human interference in their meditations. Some are said to have mastered the practice of *tumo*: controlling their body temperature at will by the force of mind power. They are said to be able to withstand even the most ferocious winter weather without any trace of frostbite simply by thinking themselves warm.

Another possible suspect is the exceptionally rare subspecies of the Asiatic brown bear that is usually called the Himalayan Bear. This is known to be more likely to walk upright on its hind legs than other types of bear. It has been observed doing so for some distance when it has wanted to keep its head high up to observe something.

If the Yeti is, in fact, an unrecognized species of ape then there is no lack of speculation as to what it might be. Back in 1825 the first Western person to learn of the creature thought that it was an orang-utan. That particular ape is today confined to the islands of Sumatra and Borneo, though it was previously found on nearby mainland Asia. However, it has never been found anywhere near the mountains. Nor is it large enough to be a realistic Yeti, though size apart it does seem to be a good fit for the cryptid.

The fossil record for apes, particularly those in Asia, is notoriously sparse. There are simply very few rocks of the right period to be found in the area. The few fragmentary remains that have turned up, however, show that apes were once far more widely distributed across southern Asia than they are today. During those periods of the recent past when the world's climate has been considerably warmer than it is now, apes have roamed widely across the area. It is not stretching credulity too much to suggest that a small population of one such species might have been able to survive in the remote forests of the Himalayas.

Within this context the Asian ape mentioned most often is the massive *Gigantopithecus*, which seems to have become extinct sometime around 150,000 years ago – or perhaps rather more recently. This ape lived across India, Southeast Asia and southern China. Fossils of the ape are rare and consist only of a handful of teeth and a couple of jaws. So far as the creature can be reconstructed from these sparse remains, it was massive. It was about 9 feet (273 cm) tall if it chose to stand on its hind legs, though it is usually considered to have spent most of its time on four legs like a modern gorilla. Its teeth indicate that it was primarily a vegetarian.

It must be admitted that the fossil record for *Gigantopithecus*, and for Asian apes in general, is so poor that it cannot really be used to prove anything. *Gigantopithecus*

Depiction of the huge ape Gigantopithecus *stalked by* Homo erectus *hunters in China 400,000 years ago.*

might have become extinct 150,000 years ago, the date of the most recent finds, or it might not have done. It might have been the only big ape with a wide distribution across southern Asia, or there might have been a dozen species wandering about. The Yeti might be descended from any one of these apes, or from none of them. We simply don't know.

Whatever the truth behind the Yeti might turn out to be, it is still a popular subject among cryptozoologists. On 26 September 2007 the original print of the Eric Shipton photograph that launched the Yeti into the world's media sold at auction for £3,600.

7 The Maricoxi

Primate Cryptids

In recent years the word 'Maricoxi' has become a generic term for any of the cryptid primates that are rumoured to live in South America – especially in the rain forests and jungles of the tropical regions. In fact several primate cryptids are said to live in the continent, going by such names as Aluxes, Goazis, Aigypans, Vasitris, Matuyus, Curupiras, Curinqueans, Didi, Mono Grande and Mapinguary. However, whether or not each name indicates a different cryptid is unclear. Some or all of the names might refer to the same creature.

The Maricoxi themselves are, or were, supposed to be an extremely primitive tribe of hominids living in the Mato Grosso. This is a vast upland region of southern Brazil and northern Paraguay that is characterized by forest and dense stands of a viciously intertwined scrub – the 'mato' of the area's name. The area covers around 500,000 square miles and although the fringes have been cleared in recent years for soya bean farming and cattle ranching, much of the interior remains untouched.

An early photo of a jaguar hunter in the dense South American forests; it was hunters who first reported the strange ape-like creature.

It was even more remote when in 1914 Colonel Percy Fawcett pushed into the area with two English companions and a small team of local porters. Fawcett had been born in Torquay in 1867 and after a distinguished career in the British army he was hired by the Bolivian government to explore and survey its more remote regions. Other commissions from South American governments followed, so Fawcett was busily engaged in mapping large areas and establishing where vaguely defined international borders went.

On these journeys into largely unexplored regions, Fawcett was told many stories about a highly advanced civilization that had formerly ruled and controlled a huge area of the rain forest. The local tribes told him that this rich and sophisticated people had formerly ruled the less advanced peoples with an iron hand and much brutality, but that they had disappeared some generations earlier. Fawcett became convinced that there had, in the recent past, been a civilization akin to the Aztec or the Maya somewhere in the interior. By studying the stories he was told, and accounts in old books, Fawcett thought the centre of this civilization had been in the Mato Grosso.

A depiction of the South American man-ape based on eyewitness reports. Note the relatively long arms, short legs and the distinct gap between the big toe and other toes.

In 1914 he pushed into the utterly unexplored area in search of the ruins of stone cities and mighty temples. He first headed for the Cordillera dos Parecis.

After some weeks, Fawcett and his companions discovered a tribe called the Maxubi. Fawcett eagerly noted that these people were sun-worshippers and had some advanced astronomical knowledge. Believing he was close to success, he pushed on even though the Maxubi had warned him that he was entering the territory of the Maracoxi. The Maracoxi were little better than animals and were highly dangerous, he was told. Fawcett dismissed the stories as being merely a sign that the two tribes were hostile to each other.

Sounds in the undergrowth

Several days after leaving the Maxubi, Fawcett heard the sounds of humans moving about in the undergrowth around his camp at night. The intruders had gone by morning, so Fawcett pushed on. He later recorded in his diary what happened next.

'In the morning we went on and within a quarter of a mile came to a sort of palm leaf sentry-box, then another. Then all of a sudden we reached open forest. The undergrowth fell away disclosing between the tree boles a village of primitive shelters, where squatted some of the most villainous savages I have ever seen. Some were engaged in making arrows, others just idled – great ape-like brutes who looked as if they had scarcely evolved beyond the level of beasts. They were large, hairy men with exceptionally long arms and with foreheads sloping back from pronounced eye ridges, men of a very primitive kind in fact and stark naked.

I whistled and an enormous creature, hairy as a dog, leapt to his feet in the nearest shelter, fitted an arrow to his bow in a flash and came up dancing from one leg to the other till he was only four yards away. Emitting grunts that sounded "eugh, eugh, eugh" he remained there dancing and suddenly the whole forest around us was alive with these hideous ape-men, all grunting and advancing from leg to leg in the same way as they strung arrows to their bows. It looked like a very delicate situation for us and I wondered if it was the end. I made friendly overtures in the Maxubi tongue, but they paid no attention. It was as though human speech were beyond their powers of comprehension.

The creature in front of me ceased his dance, stood for a moment perfectly still and then drew his bowstring back till it was level with his ear, at the same time raising the barbed point of the six-foot arrow to the height of my chest. I looked straight into the pig-like eyes half hidden under the overhanging brows and knew that he was not going to loose that arrow yet. As deliberately as he had raised it, he now lowered the bow *and commenced once more the slow dance and the "eugh, eugh, eugh".*

A second time he raised the arrow at me and drew the bow back, and again I knew he would not shoot. It was as the Maxubis told me it would be. Again he lowered the bow and continued his dance. Then for the third time he halted and began to bring up the arrow's point. I knew he meant business this time, and drew out a Mauser pistol I had on my hip. It was a big clumsy thing of a calibre unsuitable for forest use, but I had brought it because by clipping the wooden holster to the pistol butt it became a carbine and was lighter to carry than a true rifle. It used .38 black powder shells which made a din out of all proportion to their size. I never raised it. I just pulled the trigger and banged it off into the ground at the ape-man's feet.

The effect was instantaneous. A look of complete amazement came into the hideous face, and the little eyes opened wide. He dropped his bow and arrow and sprang away as quickly as a cat to vanish behind a tree. Then the arrows began to fly. We shot off a few rounds into the branches, hoping the noise would scare the savages into a more receptive frame of mind, but they seemed in no way disposed to accept us and before anyone was hurt we gave it up as hopeless and retreated down the trail till the camp was out of sight. We were not followed, but the clamour in the village continued for a long time as we struck off northward and we fancied we still heard the "eugh, eugh, eugh" of the enraged braves.'

Other early travellers also heard stories about these people – how they had a supernaturally strong sense of smell that they used when hunting, how they killed and ate humans, how they lived underground and how they were active only at night. All the neighbouring tribes and peoples firmly agreed that the Maricoxi were very primitive and very dangerous, as well as being completely covered in hair and physically different from other tribes.

There is no reason at all to doubt that Fawcett encountered these Maricoxi in the way that he said he did. He may have been fanatical about his belief in the lost Amazonian civilization, but he was a seasoned explorer and an astute observer of wildlife, geological features and flora. It seems most likely that he accurately reported his encounter with the legendary Maricoxi. He did, however, react as would a person of his time and viewed the Maricoxi through the lens of his own preconceptions. He was out looking for signs of an advanced race of astrologer princes

'A second time he raised the arrow at me and drew the bow back, and again I knew he would not shoot.'

living in stone palaces, not a bunch of hairy tribesmen. No doubt he overemphasized the primitiveness of the Maricoxi when he used phrases such as 'villainous savages' and 'ape-men', but that does not mean that his actual descriptions are wrong.

Stripped of his emotive adjectives, Fawcett's descriptions are of a fully human creature, but one with some markedly different physical characteristics. The most striking of these are thick hair all over the body, heavy brow ridges and a forehead sloping backwards. None of these are typical of *Homo sapiens sapiens*, the subspecies to which we belong. It must be admitted, however, that we really do not know at what point in our evolution we humans lost our hairy covering. That subspecies evolved somewhere in northeast Africa around 130,000 years ago and then spread out across the world. The rate at which fully modern humans spread and when they arrived in different areas is a matter of some conjecture.

What is not in doubt is that in most areas they ousted older forms of human beings. In Europe, the Neanderthal people had existed for many tens of thousands of years before fully modern humans arrived and drove them to extinction, though there may have been some limited interbreeding.

These Neanderthals are generally classed as another species of modern human, *Homo sapiens neanderthalensis*. They were originally from the same species as ourselves, but they had markedly different physical characteristics that seem to have been linked to surviving in an Ice Age environment. For instance, they had more robust bodies, bigger noses, heavy brow ridges and skulls more elongated front to back than ours. Their average skull size was, however, the same as ours and there is no reason to believe that they were any less intelligent than ourselves.

In Southeast Asia it seems to have been humans of a different species, *Homo erectus*, that were ousted when fully modern humans arrived about 90,000 years ago or so. This species had a smaller brain capacity and the tools that they made were rather more primitive than those used by modern humans – there is, for instance, no evidence that they ever mastered the making of bows, arrows or even hafted axes. They did, however, use fire for warmth and cooking. Their heads were smaller with extremely heavy brow ridges and a forehead that sloped back so severely that it almost did not exist.

In the Americas the situation is rather obscure. No fossils of any form of human have ever been found that predate the arrival of fully modern humans. That does not mean that no forms of humans lived there before that time, merely that no fossil trace has been found of them. Given the vagaries of fossil formation and the paucity of rocks of the correct age this is perhaps not surprising. It may well be that some form of early human got to America across a land bridge from Asia at some point in the remote past.

The description given of the Maricoxi of the Mato Grosso would certainly fit this scenario. It might be unlikely that a small tribe of an earlier form of the genus *Homo* has survived, but it is not impossible given the relatively late arrival of fully modern humans in the Americas. If an isolated band of *Homo erectus*, or some primitive subspecies of *Homo sapiens*, were to survive anywhere, it would be in a place that is remote from the point of entry of fully modern humans and in an environment where a limited stone tool kit might not be a great hindrance to survival. The forests of South America fit both bills.

Outside the Mato Grosso, hairy humans have been reported from the forests that blanket the eastern slopes of the lower Andes in Colombia and Ecuador. There they are known as the Shiru, but otherwise they seem very similar to the Maricoxi. Reports are sparse, however. Rather better known are the Vasitri of the Orinoco Basin, where they are also known as the Achi or Aigypan.

The Vasitri are, like the Maricoxi, quite obviously humans because they construct huts or shelters and use weapons and tools. They are, however, covered in hair and are looked upon as primitive or animal-like. Again like the Maricoxi, they are also described as being very dangerous and willing to hunt humans. They have the additional habit of kidnapping women for breeding purposes.

The first outsider to record these stories was the great German naturalist, Baron Alexander von Humboldt, who mapped much of the Orinoco River in the early 1800s. He wrote this report.

The 19th century naturalist Alexander von Humboldt recorded tales of man-apes in South America.

'On the Orinoco, it is rumoured the existence of a hairy man of the woods

called Salvaje, that carries off women, constructs huts, and sometimes eats human flesh. The Tamanacs call him Achi, and the Maypures named him Vasitri or "great devil". The natives and the missionaries have no doubt of the existence of this man-shaped monkey, of which they entertain a singular dread. Father Gili [a local missionary] gravely relates the history of a lady in the town of San Carlos, in the Llanos of Venezuela, who much praised the gentle character and attentions of the man of the woods. She is stated to have lived several years with one in great domestic harmony, and only requested some hunters to take her back, "because she and her children (a little hairy also) were weary of living far from the church and the sacraments".'

Rather older are the reports of the Mono Grande, which translates as 'giant monkey'. As its name suggests, this beast is usually described as being a very large monkey that stands about 5 feet (152 cm) tall. It often reacts badly to humans, thrashing branches about, screaming aggressively and charging at intruders. These seem to be mere displays, however, because very few people have reported being injured by a Mono Grande.

A similar creature goes by the name of the Didi. Confusion abounds regarding these two animals and they may yet turn out to be the same thing. Both live in the same area, the dense forests of northern South America and both are about the same size and have similar habits. The key difference is that the Mono Grande has a short tail, while the Didi has no tail at all. Cryptozoologists generally view the former as a form of monkey and the latter as an ape. However, the Didi may not be an ape, as such, but a monkey that has evolved into a tailless form. The truth will not be known until a skeleton can be obtained and studied.

> 'The natives and the missionaries have no doubt of the existence of this man-shaped monkey, of which they entertain a singular dread. Father Gili [a local missionary] gravely relates the history of a lady in the town of San Carlos, in the Llanos of Venezuela, who much praised the gentle character and attentions of the man of the woods.'

The two creatures will be treated here as if they are one cryptid that has been reported in different ways by witnesses and observers. However, it may turn out that there really are two quite distinct, though very similar cryptid primates in this region – one that has a tail and one that does not.

A book written in 1553 by the Spanish explorer Pedro de Cieza de León features the first written report of a Mono Grande. He mentioned that the local tribesmen told him about this creature, but that he never saw one himself. In 1769 the naturalist Edward Bancroft wrote *An Essay on the Natural History of Guiana* in which he mentions local tales of a hairy 5-foot-tall (152 cm) ape.

'It is much larger than either the African ape [chimpanzee] or the Oriental ape [orang-utan], if the accounts of the natives may be relied upon. They are represented by the Indians as being near 5 feet [152 cm] in height, maintaining an erect position and having a human form, thinly covered with short black hair, but I suspect that their height has been augmented by the fears of the Indians who greatly dread them.'

A melancholy whistle

In 1860 another British naturalist, Philip Gosse, also picked up the tales but he thought that they related to an ape. 'There may exist a large anthropoid ape, not yet recognized by zoologists', he concluded.

Eight years later Charles Brown was on the Upper Mazaruni when he heard a most peculiar animal call. He described it as follows:

'... a long, loud and most melancholy whistle. Two or three times the whistle was repeated, sounding like that made by a human being, beginning in a high key and dying slowly and gradually away into a low one.'

Brown asked his local porters what had made the cry. They told him that it was the Didi, which they described as 'a short, thickset and powerful wild man whose body is covered with hair and who lives in the forest'. Brown later met a man who had blundered across a male and a female Didi when out chopping timber one day. They had attacked him, scratching him badly, but he had defended himself with his axe and they had fled.

In 1910 came the first reported sighting of the elusive ape or giant monkey. A British gold prospector named Haines came out of the forests and said that he had encountered a pair of hairy apes as big as a man.

Haines said that when he first saw them the two creatures had been squatting down, but they had stood up when they saw him. The creatures were only a few feet away along the forest path when Haines strode round a corner. They watched him carefully for a moment and then backed off into the undergrowth while still keeping their eyes fixed on him. After they disappeared from view they seemed to rush off.

Ten years later another European saw the creature in the forests, and this time he got a photograph of it. Like the Patterson movie of an alleged Sasquatch, this photograph has become a classic of cryptozoology, one that has thrown up as many disputes as answers.

Dead animal

François de Loys was a Swiss geologist who in 1917 was hired to explore the Sierra de Perijaa area along the Colombian–Venezuela border. Part of his task was to demarcate the border, but mostly he was to prospect for the oil, gas and other natural resources that were thought to be in the area. Very definitely in the area were the Motilone, a tribe that had previously shown itself to be violently opposed to European intrusions. De Loys took with him a team made up of geologists, surveyors, armed guards and porters. He did not take naturalists because he did not need any for the task of oil prospecting.

> The creatures were screaming, shouting and thrashing at the bushes. They then tore branches off the undergrowth and started brandishing them overhead as if they were weapons.

By 1920 the team were camped near the Tarra River, some miles southwest of Maracaibo. Two large animals were seen approaching the camp through the undergrowth. De Loys at first thought that they were bears, but then he saw that they were more like very large monkeys. They seemed to be extremely angry with the humans. The creatures were screaming, shouting and thrashing at the bushes. They then tore branches off the undergrowth and started brandishing them overhead as if they were weapons. Working themselves up into a pitch of fury, the two creatures then defecated into their hands and hurled the filth at the humans. Worried, de Loys and two other men picked up their rifles, scanning the surrounding jungle for signs of other angry giant monkeys. One of the creatures then dashed towards the humans. De Loys fired, dropping the animal dead in its tracks. The other creature fled into the undergrowth and vanished from sight.

De Loys and his team picked up the dead animal and carried it back to camp. They measured it and studied it thoroughly. The creature was 5 feet 2 inches (157 cm) from its feet to the top of the head. It had no tail and its limbs were stout and muscular compared to those of most monkeys, while its body was thinner from the front to the back than he had expected. The creature had 32 teeth. Having taken these

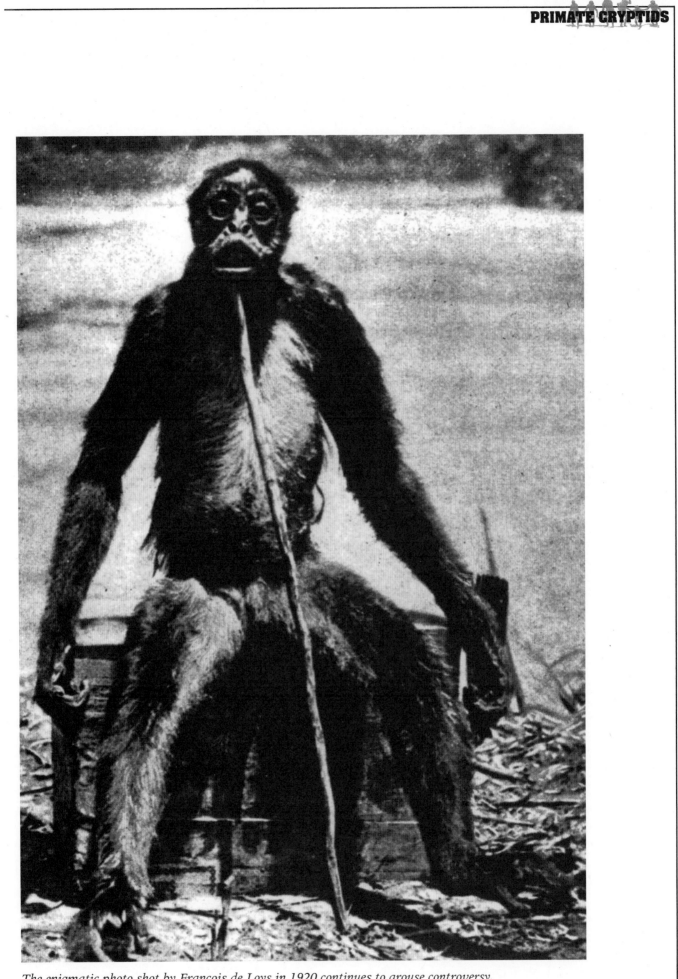

The enigmatic photo shot by François de Loys in 1920 continues to arouse controversy.

measurements, de Loys sat the creature on a wooden storage crate, propped it upright with a stick and took its photograph.

At the time of the incident de Loys questioned his porters, who all came from the coastal regions. They said that they had no idea what the creature was, but everyone agreed it was some sort of monkey. The beast was then skinned by the expedition cook, who was accustomed to dealing with all sorts of wild animals that had been shot for food. He cut off the head, boiled it to remove the flesh and kept the skull. Unfortunately the canoe which was carrying the skin and the skull overturned some weeks later and both items were lost to posterity.

> He cut off the head, boiled it to remove the flesh and kept the skull. Unfortunately the canoe carrying the skin and the skull overturned some weeks later and both items were lost…

De Loys completed his mission later that year, wrote up his geological notes for his employers and went back home to Europe. Once there he embarked on other geological work, but made no secret of the fact that he had kept voluminous notes during his South American journeys. They covered local wildlife, local tribes and other matters and several people came to inspect his notes for their own research. In 1929 the anthropologist Professor Georges Montandon visited de Loys to research South American tribes. As he flicked through de Loys' notes he spotted the photograph of the mystery monkey and asked what it was. De Loys retold the story of the encounter.

Montandon realized that the creature, as described by de Loys, was completely unknown to science. More strikingly, if the beast turned out to be an ape it would be a real landmark because no apes were known to live in the Americas. Montandon quizzed de Loys in an attempt to extract all the details he could recall. He then studied de Loys' notes assiduously, while constantly referring to the photograph. Finally Montandon published a description of the animal in the *Journal de la Société des Américanistes* and gave a talk to the French Academy of Sciences. He gave the creature the scientific name of *Ameranthropoides loysi*, meaning Loys' American Ape.

By giving the creature this name, Montandon did himself no service. The idea of there being an ape in America was opposed by nearly every zoologist of any repute. The furore that followed not only cast doubt on the already questionable identification of the animal as an ape, but went on to question the reality of the animal itself. Sir Arthur Keith, a prominent anthropologist, accused de Loys of lying. Keith suggested that the photo was of a perfectly normal spider monkey, with its tail hidden out of sight. He also pointed out that all known South American monkeys have 36 teeth, not 32. So well-respected was Keith, and so apparently ridiculous the idea of an American ape, that the subject appeared closed.

De Loys, needless to say, was furious. He denied lying and denied trickery. He repeatedly stated that at the time of the encounter he, as a geologist, had no idea that the presence of a large tailless primate was as remarkable as it turned out to be. He thought the beast was somewhat unusual, which is why he photographed it and measured it so carefully. If he had known how unusual the beast was he would have taken more photographs and tried to preserve its skeleton. In vain did de Loys claim to have done his best. The zoological world wasn't interested. De Loys gave up and went back to geology.

Reappraisal

In the intervening years there has been a reappraisal of the photo and de Loys' claims. As Keith suggested, the animal in the photograph does indeed look very much like a spider monkey. In particular it looks a bit like an Ateles spider monkey. For instance, the shape of the nose and the mouth are particularly distinctive, the nostrils being wide apart and separated by a flat area. The general proportions of the limbs and the arrangement of the toes and the fingers are also typical of spider monkeys. However, there are differences. The face of the mystery animal is a rounded oval, not the roughly triangular shape more usual in spider monkeys.

There is also the creature's size. The crate on which it is photographed is a standard one for the time, and those crates were all 18 inches (50 cm) high. Since the creature is just over three times the height of the crate, that would make it just over 5 feet (152 cm) tall. De Loys said it was 5 feet 2 inches (157 cm) tall, so he would seem to have been vindicated on this point.

There is no way of knowing from the photograph whether the creature had a tail, nor does the photograph show the number of teeth. There is only the word of de Loys to trust on either point. However, subsequent studies of spider monkeys have shown that

> There is also the creature's size. The crate on which it is photographed is a standard one for the time, and those crates were all 18 inches (50 cm) high. Since the creature is just over three times the height of the crate, that would make it just over 5 feet (152 cm) tall.

although they generally have 36 teeth, it is not at all unusual for individuals to have 34 or 32, because the third molar does not always grow. De Loys might be proved right. At the very least, what he said no longer appears as ridiculous as it did when Sir Arthur Keith wrote his damning critique. Whatever the case, sightings of the creature have continued.

In 1930 a hunter named Inocencio was out near the headwaters of the Urubu River. On one occasion he found himself unable to get back to camp before dark. Having seen recent signs of jaguar, Inocencio climbed a tree and settled himself into a fork so that he could see the ground around quite clearly. Then he loaded his gun and settled down for a sleepless night. About three hours after sunset Inocencio hear a cry that sounded almost human. Some time later he heard it again: it now sounded closer. Then it came a third time, this time much closer. Inocencio was by now a bit alarmed because he did not recognize the call at all. Then came the sound of a large animal moving cautiously through the undergrowth.

> After turning its head to stare at Inocencio it tipped its head back and let rip a terrific roaring sound. Inocencio fired and the creature again roared loudly and started running forwards as if determined to attack.

Looking in the direction from which the sound had come, Inocencio saw a creature moving beside a fallen samaumeira tree. It then stepped out into the starlight. The figure was that of a thickset being that stood upright like a man, but was somehow different. After turning its head to stare at Inocencio it tipped its head back and let rip a terrific roaring sound. Inocencio fired and the creature again roared loudly and started running forwards as if determined to attack. Inocencio shot again, and this time he seemed to hit the creature which sprang backwards. It fled back to the samaumeira tree and disappeared into the inky shadows, where it began growling and roaring. Inocencio fired for a third time, aiming blindly towards the tree. At this, the creature fell silent then roared again, but from further off. The noises continued to retreat until they finally faded out of earshot.

Curious stink

When dawn arrived Inocencio clambered down. He found the clearing around the fallen tree spattered with blood, but not enough to indicate that the mysterious creature had been fatally wounded. Many branches were broken or bent and there was a curious stink that Inocencio did not recognize.

In 1980 Fernando Nives was out hunting near Puerto Ayacucho on the Orinoco when he spotted three giant monkeys on the banks of the river. Each one was about 5 feet (152 cm) tall and covered in reddish-brown hair. Five years later Ecuadorian botanist Benigno Malo was in the dense forests looking for fungi when he saw a large ape-like creature coming towards him. It was over 4 feet (122 cm) tall and it looked rather like a chimpanzee. When it spotted Malo it made off.

Sightings by locals are numerous, but they cause little comment because the witnesses come from a culture where the reality of the creature is fully accepted. Only rarely do such cases get recorded. In 1990 Marc Miller and his daughter Khryztian organized a five-strong expedition up the Ventuari and Orinoco Rivers and their assorted tributaries in order to investigate the reports. They took with them not only the de Loys photo, but also photographs of spider monkeys, chimpanzees, gorillas and other primates. The plan was to find people who had seen the mystery giant monkey-ape, collect detailed accounts and then show them the photographs to see if they could identify what they had seen.

The expedition collected a number of eyewitness reports and managed to put together a picture of a giant monkey that tallied well with the de Loys photograph. Standing about 5 feet (152 cm) tall, it is covered in reddish-brown hair and it has arms that reach down to its knees. It eats fruits, particularly the fruits of the chonta palm, and is found most often in the hills at altitudes of over 2,000 feet. The creature is not common, but neither is it particularly rare. It seems to be wary of humans and while it will usually flee it might become aggressive if cornered.

The Millers may have returned from the dense forests certain of the reality of the giant monkey or ape, but the scientific establishment remains unconvinced.

8 Asian Wild Men

Creature of Many Names

There have been hundreds of reports coming out of Central Asia about a creature that is neither fully human nor entirely animal. It goes by many names, depending on the language of the humans who encounter it. Among the assorted dialect terms for this wild man are Abnuaaya, Barmanu, Bekk-Bok, Biabin-Guli, Gul-Biavan, Guli-Avan, Golub-Yavan, Kaptar, Kra-Dhan, Ksy Gyik, Mirygdy, Mulen and Voita. Because the study of this creature has moved out of folklore and into science, a more accepted general term has been needed to cut through the confusion. Those studying reports from China tend to call the beast the Yeren, while those looking at reports from Mongolia and what used to be the Soviet Union call it Almas, or sometimes Almasti.

The problems of studying the Almas – or the Yeren – have been compounded by the inaccessibility of the places in which it is said to live. The largest of these are the forested mountains and uplands around the Tien Shan mountain range that straddles the borders of Russia, Mongolia and China. Reports also come from the mountains of China's Hubei Province as well as the more remote regions of the Caucasus Mountains. All of these areas are far away, difficult to reach and bereft of any good roads. As if that were not enough, they lie in countries that for most of the 20th century were suspicious of foreigners – especially those wanting to travel to remote areas for obscure reasons.

It is often the case that some governments do not grant access to outsiders. The problems that these regimes can cause cryptozoology researchers can be gauged by the life of Badzare Baradyine, a leading Mongolian zoologist. Not only did Baradyine see an Almas himself, he also collected a huge amount of material on the creature.

> Baradyine was promptly arrested by the Soviets, then put up against a wall and shot. His vast collection of zoological data and specimens was confiscated and dispersed.

Unfortunately he then got involved in a campaign that aimed to give the supposedly independent Mongolia greater freedom from the oppressive Soviet regime. He was promptly arrested by the Soviets, then put up against a wall and shot. His vast collection of zoological data and specimens – including his work on the Almas – was confiscated and dispersed among various Soviet institutions, much of it being lost along the way.

Even now in the 21st century it involves a major effort to obtain permission to visit the areas where the Almas, or the Yeren, is reported to live. There then follows a

The Yeren appear to be considerably more ape-like than the Almas of Mongolia and Asiatic Russia.

The Almas goes by many different names and has even been reported as wearing rudimentary clothing.

physical endurance test to get to the remote regions. And all of this costs a huge amount of money.

As a result much of the evidence for the existence of this enigmatic creature relies on translations of media reports or scientific journals that have filtered out of the countries concerned. Putting these together can be a time-consuming and frustrating task that does not guarantee any firm answers.

Mongolian Sightings

One of the first outsiders to take an interest in the Almas-Yeren was the Russian doctor Ivan Ivlov, who then publicized his findings. Ivlov had been sent by the Soviet regime to minister to children in Mongolia, as part of a goodwill mission to strengthen bonds between the two Communist nations. In the autumn of 1963 he was travelling through the Altai Mountains, a northern spur of the Tien Shan, along with some local Mongolians who were acting as guides and transporting his medical equipment. Suddenly spotting three figures some distance away on a mountain slope. Ivlov got out his binoculars to get a better view. He saw that the shape of the figures, and the way they moved, was human but that they were covered in hair. There was a male, a slightly smaller female and a child. The creatures seemed to be digging, perhaps for roots to eat. When they saw Ivlov and his caravan the figures moved off. They rounded a rock crag and so disappeared from sight. Ivlov was puzzled and turned to his Mongolian companions. They told him that the figures were wild men. They explained that the wild men were not really humans, but were more like animals.

Ivlov was intrigued and throughout the rest of his journey he asked his patients about these mysterious wild men. He learned that the local herdsmen did not think that the human-like creatures were at all mysterious or unusual: they were just another part of the local wildlife.

One patient told Ivlov of the time an Almas male had scooped up a juvenile when it spotted the Mongolian approaching. As the adult Almas strode off, the youngster peered over its shoulder at the human, then stuck its tongue out and made faces – a remarkably human response.

Ivlov came out of Mongolia with his stories just as interest in the Himalayan Yeti was at a peak. At first his tales of an upright-walking, human-like creature in the more northern mountain range were thought to be just another report of a Yeti, albeit from a

The Katun River as it flows through the remote Altai Mountains, an area which is thought to be the stronghold of the Almas.

different area. As researchers began looking into the subject, however, it gradually emerged that the Almas or Yeren was far more like a human than was the basically ape-like Yeti. It also transpired that the wild men had a rather longer history of encounters with humans than did the Yeti, the Sasquatch or any other type of cryptid primate.

The oldest written reference to an Asian wild man so far discovered comes from the book written in the 1430s by a Bavarian nobleman called Hans Schiltberger. Schiltberger had the misfortune to be captured in battle by Mongols of the Golden Horde, then sold as a slave to Egidi, a merchant from Mongolia. After extensive travels through the world of the Mongol hordes that then ruled most of Asia, Schiltberger eventually got back to Europe, where he was bought by a Christian and set free to return home. He wrote up his memoirs and included the following section when talking about the Tien Shan.

'In the mountains live wild people, who have nothing in common with normal human beings. A pelt of fur covers the entire body of these creatures. Only the hands and face are

free of hair. They run around the hills like animals and eat foliage and grass and whatever else they can find. The lord of the territory made Egidi a present of two of these forest people, a man and a woman. They had been caught in the wilderness along with three untamed horses the size of asses and some other animals not found in our lands and which I cannot therefore put a name to.'

From what he says elsewhere, the wild horses that Schiltberger refers to were the species now known as Przewalski's wild horse. These animals do, indeed, live in the foothills of the Tien Shan just as Schiltberger claimed, so he probably remembered correctly about the 'forest people'.

Published in the Qing dynasty in around the year 1664 was a book entitled *The Mirror of Medicine*. A compendium of wild animals to be found in northern China and Mongolia, it gave the ways in which their flesh, bones or other parts could be used in traditional medicine. Among all the assorted birds, fish and mammals that are unquestionably real creatures was included the 'wild man'. According to the text:

'The wild man lives in the northern mountains and his origins are like that of the bear. His body resembles that of a man and he has enormous strength. His meat may be eaten to treat mental disease. His gall cures jaundice.'

Alongside the text was a small illustration. It showed a basically human figure standing on a rock with its left arm upraised. The entire body of the creature, except for its feet and hands, was shown covered in dense fur. Even the eyes and the mouth were surrounded by hair. As with the patients of Ivlov, the writer of the book was referring to the wild man as if he were nothing out of the way or extraordinary.

An Almas woman was apparently captured in the 1890s or thereabouts. In 1910 a Kazakh herdsmen told Russian zoologist V.A. Khaklov that he recalled having seen a wild woman in his youth. He said that she had been captured by some farmers and was being kept chained up when he saw her. The herdsman said that the woman was usually quiet, but would screech and bare her teeth if approached. He said that she had a most peculiar way of lying down to sleep. She rested on her knees and elbows with her forehead on the ground and with her hands folded over the back of her head. The herdsman recalled that the wild woman ate raw meat and vegetables and that when drinking she would lap like a dog. She was apparently released after a few days and fled back to the forests.

In 1907 Professor Tsyben Zhamtsarano, a Mongol who had been educated in St Petersburg, found himself sentenced to indefinite internal exile for getting involved in revolutionary political activity. To his delight he found that he had been exiled to his homeland in the far east of the Russian Empire. He stayed there even after the Soviet Union replaced the Tsarist regime, continuing his scholarly work in the quiet, remote area. Among the subjects he investigated were the Almas.

Zhamtsarano interviewed dozens of Mongolian nomads who claimed to have encountered the wild men. He made detailed notes of their reports and got a local artist to work with the nomads to produce a series of pictures of the creatures that they had seen. He also drew up a large map of the Tien Shan region and marked on it each sighting, together with the date it was made. He returned to Leningrad, as St Petersburg had then become, in 1928. When he died in 1940 his archives were taken by the Leningrad Institute of Oriental Studies. So far as is known they were destroyed during the German siege of Leningrad in 1941–42.

In the 1960s, one of Zhamtsarano's research assistants, Dordji Meiren, was asked what he could remember of the Almas data. This had not been his speciality, but he did remember some of the things that Zhamtsarano had told him and he also recalled some details of the marked-up map. He recollected that reports had been particularly numerous in the Gourban Bogdin, Chardzyn and Alachan districts, but had also been made from the Khalkha, Galbin, Khovd and Dzakh Soudjin regions. He said that Zhamtsarano believed that the numbers of reports had declined drastically after about 1890 and that by 1925 the Almas appeared to have become extinct across as much as half of its range.

The one thing that Meiren did recall very clearly was being shown a skin of an Almas male. It seemed to be that of a human a little over 5 feet (152 cm) tall, except that it was covered in dense reddish-brown curly hair. The hair on the scalp was much longer and densely matted but the face was hairless around the eyes and the mouth. Short, curly hair grew on the cheeks and the forehead. The fingers and toes, Meiren said, carried nails that looked identical to those of a human. He did not know what had become of the hide.

The mystery resurfaced in 1980. A man working for the Mongolian government was travelling through Bulgan when he came across a dead body. At first he took it to be that of a human. Later on he recorded the following statement:

'I approached and saw a hairy corpse of a robust humanlike creature dried and half-buried by sand. I had never seen such a humanlike being before covered by camel-colour

In 1941 Red Army troops captured a creature in far-flung forests that was more ape than man.

Nikolai Przhevalsky (1839–88) was a Russian geographer and explorer of eastern and central Asia. He was the first man to send back reports of sub-human hominids there.

brownish-yellow short hairs and I recoiled, although in my native land in Sinkiang I had seen many dead men killed in battle. The dead thing was not a bear or ape and at the same time it was not a man like Mongol or Kazakh or Chinese and Russian. The hairs of its head were longer than on its body. The skin was darkened and shrivelled like a hide of a dead camel.'

Then, in 1992, the first serious expedition to investigate the Almas was led into the Tien Shan area by Dr Marie-Jeanne Koffman, a Russian anatomist and mountain climber. The team was a joint French–Russian affair that spent some weeks in the remote region. During that time the expedition collected more than 500 eyewitness accounts, including descriptions of Almas families. Although no Almas was captured, nor even seen by expedition members, they did come back with some droppings and hairs that the locals said had come from the Almas. Although the hairs could not be matched to any known animal they might have come from a primate. The droppings contained food remains that showed that the animal that had made them was omnivorous, but in shape and texture they were quite unlike those of a bear – the only large omnivore known to live in the area.

Armed with clubs

The Pamir Mountains lie to the southwest of the Tien Shan and tales of the Almas have come from there also. One of the earliest reports to come out of the region was that of Major General Mikhail Topilski. He was commanding a cavalry regiment in the Red Army during the civil war that wracked the Russian Empire after the Communist Revolution of 1917. In 1925 Topilski and his men were given the task of hunting down anti-Communist forces in the Pamirs.

Topilski and his men had been tracking a group of a dozen or so fugitives – Topilski called them 'bandits' – for some time when they heard gunshots. Three of the enemy were running towards them, so the Red Army men opened fire, killing two and wounding the third. The wounded man turned out to be an Uzbek from Samarkand. When questioned he said that he and his companions had not been attacking Topilski's unit but had been fleeing an even worse danger – gigantic hairy men who were armed with clubs.

At first Topilski did not believe the Uzbek, but the wounded man then showed him the site of the fight, a cave beside a glacier. The bodies of the five 'bandits' were found and so was the body of one of the 'hairy giants'. Topilski's report continued:

'The body had three bullet wounds. Not far off we found a stick made of very hard wood, though it cannot be stated for certain that it belonged to the creature. At first glance I thought the body was that of an ape. It was covered with hair all over. But I knew there were no apes in the Pamirs. Also, the body itself looked very much like that of a man. We tried pulling the hair, to see if it was just a hide used for disguise, but found that it was the creature's own natural hair. We turned the body over several times on its back and its front and measured it. Our doctor (who was killed later the same year) made a long and thorough inspection of the body, and it was clear that it was not a human.

The body belonged to a male creature 170 cm [5 feet 8 inches] tall, elderly or even old judging by the greyish colour of the hair in places. The chest was covered by brownish hair and the belly with greyish hair. The hair was longer but sparser on the chest but short and thick on the belly. In general the hair was very thick, without any underfur. There was least hair on the buttocks, from which fat our doctor deduced that the creature sat like a human being. There was most hair on the hips. The knees were completely bare of hair and had callous growths on them. The whole foot including the sole was quite hairless and was covered by hard brown skin. The hair got thinner near the hand and the palms had none at all, but only callous skin.

The colour of the face was dark, and the creature had neither beard nor moustache. The temples were bald and the back of the head was covered by thick, matted hair. The dead creature lay with its eyes open and its teeth bared. The eyes were dark and the teeth were large and even and shaped like human teeth. The forehead was slanting and the eyebrows were very powerful. The protruding jaw bones made the face resemble the Mongol type of face. The nose was flat with a deeply sunk bridge. The ears were hairless and looked a little more pointed than a human being's with a longer lobe. The lower jaw was very massive.

The creature had a very powerful chest and well developed muscles. We didn't find any important anatomical difference between it and man. The genitalia were like a man's. The arms were of normal length, the hands were slightly wider and the feet much wider and shorter than a man's.'

Some years later, in 1948, M.A. Stonin, a geologist, was prospecting near Tien Shan. One morning he awoke to cries by his guides that the horses were being stolen. Stonin grabbed his rifle and headed outside to find a figure standing by the horses. It had long red hair all over its body. The creature moved off at Stonin's shouts and he chased after it. It was so man-like, though, that Stonin couldn't bring himself to shoot it and the thing escaped.

Reports from China

Reports from the Chinese mountain forests are rarer, though that may have as much to do with political events in China as with the numbers of actual encounters. Again, records of the wild men go back a long way. Li Yanshow, a 9th century historian, stated that the forests of Hubei province sheltered a band of wildmen. In the 18th century, the Chinese poet Yuan Mei wrote about creatures in the wild regions of Shanxi province, calling them 'monkeylike, yet not monkeylike'.

Wang Zelin, a graduate of the biology department of Northwestern University in Chicago, USA, saw the corpse of one of these creatures in 1940. He was driving to Tianshui, in Gansu Province, when he heard gunfire and then came across a group of soldiers standing around a strange body. It was a female human-like creature, about 6 feet 6 inches (197 cm) tall and covered with a coat of thick greyish-red hair about one and a quarter inches (3 cm) long. The hair on its head was about a foot (30 cm) long but the hair on its face was shorter. Its cheek bones were prominent and its lips jutted out.

Then, in 1957, a middle-school teacher of biology in Zhejiang province claimed to have obtained the hands and feet of a 'man-bear' killed by local peasants. He believed that they belonged to a primate since they looked like the hands of an ape or a large monkey. After much thought he decided that they might possibly belong to an enormous monkey of some unknown kind.

In June 1997 the Xinhua News Agency of China issued the following report to the international media:

'"Hundreds of very large footprints resembling those of a man – but much larger – have been seen in the forests of the mountainous Shennongjia National Park in central Hubei province," says Wang Fangchen, head of the privately run Committee for Research on Strange and Rare Creatures.

"We have made preliminary conclusions that they were left by two animals walking on two legs," said Wang, who has been hunting for the fabled creature for several years.

The famous Yeren Cave in the Hubei Mountains of China, said to be favoured by the man-apes.

"The biggest footprint is 37 centimetres [15 inches] long, very similar to that of a man but is quite [a bit] larger than a man's, and is different from the footprints of a bear or any other identified animals," Wang said.'

He said he believed the creature that made the footprints weighed about 440 pounds. Wang had led a team of 30 scientists on a fruitless hunt through Shennongjia the previous summer. He had vowed to resume his search for the fabled 197 cm-tall (6 feet 6 inches), red-haired, human-like creature that is part of local folklore.

Wang's team found similar footprints left by two other mysterious creatures in Shennongjia last winter. Progress toward unravelling the myth of the 'wild man' would be of great scientific significance, Wang said. But he urged caution and warned researchers not to jump to swift conclusions without hard scientific evidence.

Theories abound about the mythical creature, with some scientists speculating that if it exists it may be an unknown primate, some arguing fairly persuasively that it may be a bear or a monkey and others suggesting it could be a missing evolutionary link between ape and human.

By May 2000 the Xinhua News Agency had decided to use the American term of Bigfoot for the Yeren when it issued the following report from Wuhan:

An open-cast mine in the Hubei Mountains: is human intrusion driving the Yeren to extinction?

'"Guided tours on the periphery of Shennongjia Nature Reserve, believed home to the 'Chinese Bigfoot', will be provided in the Fall," said Wang Zhenyou, mayor of Yichang City where the Three Gorges Project is under construction.

"They will be able to visit the roads where local residents have reportedly seen Bigfoot, but tourists will not be allowed to go further into the Nature Reserve," Wang said.

The guided tours become a part of the Yangtze Three Gorges International Tourism Festival in Yichang City, in central China's Hubei Province from September 30 to October 30.'

A team of paleoanthropologists from Beijing, together with local researchers and reporters, discovered footprints that were 16 inches (40 cm) long, brown hair and chewed corn cobs in Shennongjia last October. The possibility that it was a bear has been ruled out by Yuan Zhenxin, a well-known paleoanthropologist from the Chinese Academy of Sciences (CAS).

Life sciences professor Pan Wenshi from Beijing University visited the Nature Reserve several years ago. He believed that it was not an ideal living environment for quadrumana (primates with four hands) because of frequent human activities and the shortage of broad-leaved trees and berries in the forest.

Another scientist, Wang Fangchen, head of the Committee for Search for Rare Animals and Plants, said that repeated attempts to track down Bigfoot have been disappointing. However, a few scientists do believe in the possibility that such a half-man, half-ape creature still exists in the forests of China. It is reported that there have been sightings of Bigfoot in Tibet Autonomous Region in southwest China.

Reports from the Caucasus

Although the majority of Almas reports come from the Tien Shan and nearby regions, others come from the Caucasus. One of the first reports to made by an outsider was in 1899 when the Russian zoologist K.A. Satunin was travelling through the Talysh hills of Georgia. At dusk he saw a human-like figure that seemed to be covered in hair. The sighting lasted only a few seconds before the creature dashed off into dense undergrowth, but Satunin's guides told him that the creature had been a forest woman – a Biaban Guli or Kaptar.

According to a later account a Kaptar woman was captured alive in the Caucasus Mountains sometime around 1840. She was described as being covered all over in dark red-brown hair, beneath which she had an equally dark skin. Her body was broad and muscular, as were her limbs and she had particularly big hands. Hair also covered her head, although it was much longer over her scalp, and her forehead sloped back sharply from thick eyebrows. The Kaptar woman could not talk and never learned to speak the local language, though she could make herself understood at a fairly basic level with hand gestures. She seemed to call herself something that sounded like 'Zana', so that was the name that she was given.

> The Kaptar woman could not talk and never learned to speak the local language, though she could make herself understood at a fairly basic level with hand gestures.

Over the years that followed Zana was sold or given to various owners: one of them was a nobleman who was interested in wildlife. She ate human food, and greatly enjoyed alcohol which she drank to excess whenever she could. When drunk she was very amorous and as a result she gave birth to six children. The first two died after Zana washed them immediately after birth in a cold stream, but the others survived when the local women prevented her from plunging them into the same cold water. These four children, two boys and two girls, grew up to be quite normal, except that they inherited their mother's dark skin and powerful physique. Zana died in the 1880s.

In 1964 the Russian historian Boris Porshnev visited the town of Tkvartcheli, where two of Zana's grandsons were working in a local mine. He wrote:

'From the moment I saw Zana's grandchildren, I was impressed by their dark skin and negroid looks. Shalikula, the grandson, has unusually powerful jaw muscles, and he can pick up a chair, with a man sitting on it, with his teeth.'

They had a picture of their father, Khvit, the younger of Zana's two sons. He had died aged around 70 in the 1950s. The picture showed a man with excessively curly hair, prominent lips and heavy eyebrows. Several elderly people told Porshnev that they remembered Zana well and had attended her funeral.

The captured woman was able to breed with her captors... the ability to produce offspring that are able to breed is restricted to members of the same species.

Porshnev tried to find Zana's remains in the local cemetery, but was frustrated by the fact that individual graves were not marked, only the area in which the members of families were interred. They found one broken skull that had strong brow ridges and an overall elongated shape, but were not sure what to make of it. Porshnev guessed it might have belonged to one of Zana's children.

This incident is intriguing because of the fact that the captured woman was able to breed with her captors. Zoologically, the ability to breed and produce offspring that are themselves able to breed is restricted to members of the same species. Lions cannot mate with wolves to produce young. It is true that some closely related species can interbreed. Lions and tigers can produce young, as can donkeys and horses, but these offspring are invariably sterile and unable to produce young themselves.

The fact that Zana was able to have young by her captors and that they could

Human evolution: the Yeren and Almas are reported to have a similar stance to stages two and three.

themselves have babies would indicate that whatever else she was, Zana was definitely human. Some researchers have concluded that Zana was a negro woman, perhaps a slave from Turkey who had fled over the mountains in an effort to find freedom. The local farmers are unlikely to have come across any black Africans and so may have mistaken her for some form of wild woman. Others think that the episode proves that the wild men are a type of human not too different from ourselves.

An event from 1941 has been often quoted, but its precise meaning is unclear. A Russian officer named Vargen Karapetyan was fighting the German invaders near Buinakst when some partisans asked him what they should do with a rather unusual prisoner. Karapetyan later wrote:

'I entered a shed with two members of the local authorities. When I asked why I had to examine the man in a cold shed and not in a warm room, I was told that the prisoner could not be kept in a warm room. He had sweated in the house so profusely that they had had to keep him in the shed. I can still see the creature as it stood before me, a male, naked and barefooted. And it was doubtlessly a man, because its entire shape was human. The chest, back, and shoulders, however, were covered with shaggy hair of a dark brown colour. This

fur of his was much like that of a bear, and 2 to 3 centimeters [1 inch] long. The fur was thinner and softer below the chest. His wrists were crude and sparsely covered with hair. The palms of his hands and the soles of his feet were free of hair. But the hair on his head reached to his shoulders partly covering his forehead. The hair on his head, moreover, felt very rough to the hand. He had no beard or moustache, though his face was completely covered with a light growth of hair. The hair around his mouth was also short and sparse. The man stood absolutely straight with his arms hanging, and his height was above the average – about 180 cm [5 feet 11 inches]. He stood before me like a giant, his mighty chest thrust forward. His fingers were thick, strong and exceptionally large. On the whole, he was considerably bigger than any of the local inhabitants. His eyes told me nothing. They were dull and empty – the eyes of an animal. And he seemed to me like an animal and nothing more.'

The male would bring fruits or roots from the forest to exchange for the trinkets and although the females or young males might approach, it was not very often.

Karapetyan had no idea what to do with the prisoner and a few days later he heard that he had escaped. However, a later report made by the Ministry of the Interior in Daghestan said that the prisoner had been executed as a deserter after being court-martialled.

In 1958 Yu Merezhinski, a professor of anthropology at the Kiev University, was in Azerbaijan collecting material when he heard about the forest men. A local hunter said that he knew of a spot where the wild men could often be found and offered to take Merezhinski there to take a photograph.

The pair trekked up into forested mountains for some miles and eventually came to a small stream. There the hunter found a spot where the stream formed a deep pool. He then ushered Merezhinski into a dense thicket and told him to sit down and wait. The hours ticked by and nothing much happened, then the hunter nudged Merezhinski and pointed. On the far side of the pool the bushes were moving. Then out stepped a curious creature that looked like a person. It was just over 5 feet (152 cm) tall and it was covered all over in short, pale hair.

Instead of taking out his camera, Merezhinski reached for his pistol. The hunter became suddenly angry, shoving Merezhinski roughly aside as he shot. Because of this, the bullet missed the hairy figure, which then darted off into the undergrowth. After leading Merezhinski back to his village, the hunter refused to have anything more to do with him.

Another researcher who was active in the 1960s was John Colarusso. After speaking at great length to Caucasian hill men he slowly became convinced of the reality of the Kaptar. He recorded several instances of men who claimed to have traded with the forest men. One hunter said that he would frequently take beads and shiny bangles or sequins with him when visiting the high valleys. These he would spread out on the ground by his camp to attract the forest men. He said that the first sign of the creatures would be when a large male was seen hovering about near the forest edge.

Then the male would come forward, while females and children could be glimpsed hiding in the undergrowth. The male would bring fruits or roots from the forest to exchange for the trinkets and although the females or young males might approach, it was not very often. None made any effort to talk to him, though they would often jabber to each other in some strange way, using hand signs and facial expressions instead. He reported that they were unaggressive, but were sly and cunning. If he did not keep his eyes open the forest people would try to steal his trinkets.

What the forest people looked like

From the accounts given by Colarusso it seemed that these forest people stood a bit over 5 feet (152 cm) tall and were covered in slightly curly brown or reddish hair, which was much longer on the top of the head. Their faces were described as being pushed forward, indicating that the chin and forehead both sloped backwards. They walked upright like men and were agile and immensely strong. The Kaptar were not aggressive, but would fight ferociously if they felt threatened or if a human got too close to a young Kaptar.

In the 1960s, Dr Kofman, who was later to investigate the Almas of Mongolia, was involved in work in Azerbaijan that touched on the Kaptar. She collected a number of sighting reports that confirmed the picture built up by Colarusso. During a lecture that she gave to the Russian Geographical Society in Moscow in March 1966, she displayed an artwork that showed what she thought the forest men looked like. One of her audience approached her a short time later with a very similar artwork, but this one did not depict a mysterious cryptid hominid from remote mountains, but was a scientific reconstruction of a Neanderthal man based on a complete skull.

Kofman then began to wonder if the Kaptar, the Almas, the Yeren and the like were isolated surviving populations of Neanderthals. The idea has since been taken up by others. Although it remains unrecognized by mainstream science it does have something to recommend it.

Have Any Neanderthals Survived?

Human evolution is a complex subject for which there is surprisingly little fossil evidence. Scientists frequently change their minds about how modern humans have evolved as new evidence is found, or old evidence is reappraised. Inevitably, there are often disputes between specialists. The general view as it currently stands is that about 5 million years ago in Africa a branch of the ape family known as the australopithecines evolved to walk upright. These creatures were not markedly more intelligent than other apes and did not use tools. About 2 million years ago one branch of the australopithecines, generally called the habilines, developed a larger brain and began making tools. Some consider these apes to have been advanced enough to be classified as humans, others do not.

Finally, about a million years ago, the first creature that is widely accepted as a human appeared. This was *Homo erectus*, which first evolved in East Africa but then spread out to live across all of Africa, Europe and Asia. The body of *Homo erectus* was very like that of a modern human, but the skull was rather different. It had a small ridge along the top for the attachment of powerful jaw muscles and a second ridge around the base of the rear. Its forehead sloped back dramatically from massive eyebrow ridges that ran straight across the face from one side to the other and its face was very wide and shallow. A feature of the lower jaw was that it lacked a chin.

The way we were

About 200,000 years ago our own species, *Homo sapiens*, appeared: again this was in East Africa. *Homo sapiens* developed into a number of different subspecies which were all basically the same animal, but with some minor differences. One of these subspecies was the Neanderthal or *Homo sapiens neanderthalensis*. Neanderthals first evolved in Europe or the Middle East about 125,000 years ago. They spread fairly rapidly west across Europe and east at least as far as the Balkhash Lake in Kazakhstan: a point midway between the Caucasus and the Tien Shan mountains.

In its general shape, the Neanderthal skull was midway between that of a fully modern human and *Homo erectus*. There was a heavy ridge of bone along the eyebrows, but it was not as pronounced as before, and it now had arches over the eyes that were something like our own. The forehead sloped back, but it was rather more upright than before and the face was less wide and heavy. However, the lower jaw still lacked a proper chin and the nasal bones indicate that the nose was fairly wide and flat. The key difference between Neanderthals and *Homo erectus* was that the Neanderthal skull contained a brain every bit as large as that of a modern human. This is demonstrated by the fact that the Neanderthals made and used tools of bone, stone and wood.

Side-branch of evolution

The Neanderthal skeleton was very similar to that of modern humans, but it was shorter, stockier and more heavily muscled. Neanderthals would have only reached a height of about 5 feet 3 inches (160 cm). Most scientists believe that the Neanderthals were a side-branch of human evolution that evolved to suit the very cold conditions of the Ice Age. The short, stocky body was better able to retain heat, while the big nose would have warmed cold air before it entered the delicate lungs. If this were the case it would have made sense for Neanderthals to have developed a thick hairy coat, but since only the bones of these humans have survived we have no way of knowing if this was or was not the case.

Finally, about a million years ago, the first creature that is widely accepted as a human appeared. This was *Homo erectus*, which first evolved in East Africa but then spread out to live across all of Africa, Europe and Asia.

Meanwhile, fully modern humans evolved in East Africa about 120,000 years ago. Sometime about 90,000 years ago – the date is unclear – this subspecies migrated out of Africa into the Middle East and then spread slowly across Asia and Europe. Later on they reached Australia and the Americas. They seem to have driven out earlier types of human rather than mixing with them. The precise timing of these migrations is unclear, but according to the archaeological evidence the last known Neanderthal population seems to have lived in southeastern Europe, perhaps as recently as about 20,000 years ago.

We know, therefore, that Neanderthals did live in the areas where Almas are reported today. We know also that in their overall appearance the Neanderthals looked very like the descriptions of the Almas that witnesses have given. What we do not know for certain is when the Neanderthals were replaced by modern humans in these areas. It is not even certain that modern humans did replace Neanderthals in all places.

It is possible that some small populations of Neanderthals, or some similar form of early modern humans, have survived into modern times in remote regions.

9 Orang Pendek

The Short Man

Somewhere in the mountainous forests of southern Sumatra is said to live the Orang Pendek – the 'short man'. The local villagers of the more densely forested regions appear to take the creature for granted, much as they do the tiger and the rhinoceros which, although rare, frequent these woods. When told that Western scientists do not recognize the Orang Pendek as a real creature, the locals are inclined to scoff.

The first reference to this creature to be written by an outsider was made in 1917 by a Dr Edward Jacobson. The good doctor wrote about the creature in a scientific journal published in the Netherlands, Sumatra then being part of the Dutch colonial empire. Jacobson said that he had been camped near Boekit Kaba when the local men he had hired to hunt meat for him came strolling in to announce that they had just passed an Orang Pendek. It had been looking for insect larvae in a fallen log. They said that the creature had run off when it had seen them and, when questioned, insisted that it did so on its hind legs.

Jacobson thought this odd because the only apes he knew of, gibbons and orang-utans, would have swung off through the trees. He went to investigate and found a footprint that looked exactly like that of a human, except that it was very small. Jacobson's letter prompted a separate report from another European living in Sumatra, L.C. Westenenk. Westenenk reported that a friend of his had been leading a gang of workmen into the forest near Loeboek Salasik to cut timber when they came across what he described as:

'*... a large creature, low on its feet which ran like a man and was about to cross the path. It was very hairy and was not an orangutan. Its face was not like an ordinary man's. It silently and gravely gave the men a disagreeable stare and ran calmly away. The workmen ran faster in the opposite direction.*'

Also joining in the correspondence was a Mr Oostingh, the manager of a coffee plantation at Dataran, who in 1917 had managed to get lost in the forest. He emerged into a clearing to discover what he took to be a man sitting with his back to him.

'*I saw that he had short hair, cut short I thought, and I suddenly realized that his neck was oddly leathery and extremely filthy. "That chap's got a very dirty and wrinkled neck," I said to myself. His body was as large as a medium-sized native's [the average height of a native Sumatran is about 5 feet 7 inches (170 cm)] and he had thick square shoulders, not sloping at all. The colour was not brown, but looked like black earth, a sort of dusty black, more grey than black.*'

The Orang Pendek is a small ape-like creature thought to exist in remote Sumatran forests.

He clearly noticed my presence. He did not so much as turn his head, but stood up on his feet. He seemed to be quite as tall as I am, 5 feet 9 inches [175 cm]. Then I saw that it was not a man, and I started back for I was not armed. The creature calmly took several paces, without the least haste, and then with his ludicrously long arm grasped a sapling which threatened to break under his weight and quietly sprang into a tree, swinging in great leaps alternately to right and to left.

It was not an orangutan, I had seen one of these large apes a short time before. It was more like a monstrously large siamang [a type of gibbon], but a siamang has long hair and there was no doubt that it had short hair. I did not see its face for it never once looked at me.'

Further sightings

It has been suggested that what Oostingh saw was, in fact, a very large siamang. The average height for these animals is about 3 feet (91 cm), but old males are known to grow rather larger. This would certainly fit the description of the creature swinging off through the trees. Other reports of the Orang Pendek usually say that it runs off on the ground.

Mr Coomans, a railway manager, continued the correspondence when he wrote of an incident near his station at Benkoelen:

'Footprints of pygmies were found. They were like a child's footprints, but broader. Later the same prints were found near Soungei Klomboek. Along this creature's path the stones had been turned over here and there as though it was looking for food beneath them.'

It was a farmer named Van Herwaarden who produced the clearest of these early reports. He was out hunting wild pigs when he saw something unusual sitting in a tree.

'My first quick look revealed nothing, but after walking round the tree again, I discovered a dark and hairy creature on a branch. The front of its body was pressed tightly against the tree. It looked as if it were trying to make itself inconspicuous and felt that it was about to be discovered.

I laid my gun on the ground and tried to get nearer the animal. I had hardly climbed 3 or 4 feet into the tree when the body above me began to move. The creature lifted itself a little from the branch and leaned over the side so that I could then see its hair, its forehead and a pair of eyes which stared at me.

Its movements had at first been slow and cautious, but as soon as the thing saw me the

A reconstruction of the sighting by Van Herwaarden of an Orang Pendek sitting eating in a tree.

A typical stretch of Sumatran rainforest which could provide suitable habitat for the Orang Pendek.

whole situation changed. It became nervous and trembled all over. In order to see it better I slid down on to the ground.

    The beast was also hairy on the front of its body, the colour there was a little lighter than on the back. The very dark hair on its head fell to just below the shoulder blades or even almost to the waist. It was fairly thick and very shaggy. The lower part of its face seemed to end in more of a point than a man's. This brown face was almost hairless, while the forehead seemed to be high rather than low. Its eyebrows were the same colour as its hair and were very bushy. The eyes were frankly moving. They were the darkest colour, very lively and like human eyes. The nose was broad with fairly large nostrils, but in no way clumsy. It reminded me a little of a negro's. Its lips were quite ordinary, but the width of its mouth was strikingly wide when open. Its canines showed clearly from time to time as its mouth twitched nervously. They seemed fairly large to me, at all events they were more developed than a man's. The incisors were regular. The colour of the teeth was yellowish white. The chin was somewhat receding. For a moment I was able to see its right ear, which was exactly like a little human ear. Its hands were slightly hairy on the back. Had it been standing, its arms would have reached to a little above its knees, they were long, but its legs seemed to me rather short. I did not see its feet, but I did see some toes which were shaped in a very normal manner. This specimen was of the female sex and about 5 feet [152 cm] in height.

> 'People may think me childish [that] when I saw its flying hair in the sights I did not pull the trigger. I suddenly felt that I was going to commit murder.'

There was nothing repulsive or ugly about the face, nor was it at all ape like, although the quick nervous movements of its eyes and mouth were very like those of a monkey in distress. I began to talk in a calm and friendly way to the beast as if I were soothing a frightened dog or horse, but it did not make much difference. When I raised my gun, I heard a plaintive "hu-hu", which was at once answered by similar calls from the forest nearby.

I laid my gun on the ground and climbed into the tree again. The beast ran very fast along a branch, then dropped 10 feet [3 m] to the ground. By the time I reached my gun it was 30 yards away and running fast, giving a sort of whistle. Many people may think me childish if I say that when I saw its flying hair in the sights I did not pull the trigger. I suddenly felt that I was going to commit murder.'

Crushing disappointment

In 1932 native hunters presented what they said was the body of a young Orang Pendek to the Sumatran newspaper the *Deli Courant*, in return for the reward that the newspaper had offered for proof of the creature's existence. The newspaper gleefully printed the story of the mystery animal's arrival, its appearance, its condition and the fact that it was being sent to Dr Dammerman of the Zoological Museum at Buitenzorg for study.

When the report came back it was a crushing disappointment. The supposed Orang Pendek juvenile was simply a hoax. A fully grown langur monkey had been shot, then had its fur trimmed to match the usual description of an Orang Pendek's hair. The nose had been stretched with a piece of wood, the teeth filed to shape and the cheekbones carefully fractured to alter their shape.

All of this had a most unfortunate effect. The Dutch colonial authorities lost all interest in this supposed rare member of Sumatra's fauna and the whole thing became something of a joke. Anyone who mentioned the subject was treated as a fool and subjected to ridicule – rather as if they had declared that they had seen Father Christmas passing by in his flying sleigh. In 1941 the island was invaded by the Japanese, then liberated in 1945 and finally returned to Dutch rule before, in 1947, joining the newly independent state of Indonesia.

The whole subject of the strange human-like ape in the southern forests got forgotten, except by the local people who claim to have come across it frequently. Then, in July 1989 a British reporter named Deborah Martyr went to Sumatra to produce some travel features. While there she went up to the Mount Kerinici area of the dense, largely unexplored rain forest to seek out animals to photograph. Her guide, a man named Jamruddin, was asked where they had to travel to see the different animals. He began by explaining where to see tigers and where they would travel to see rhinoceros and other creatures. Then, quite casually, he pointed to the area of land east of Mount Tujuh and remarked that if they had more time they could go there to see Orang Pendek, but that there was not really time and in any case the creatures were rare and very shy.

A type of gibbon?

At the time Martyr did not know about the earlier reports and thought that Jamruddin was using a local name for a type of gibbon. Gradually she realized that he and others who said that they had met the Orang Pendek were referring to something very different from the gibbons or orang-utans with which she was familiar. Back in London, Martyr researched the term and discovered the Orang Pendek was a cryptid ape supposed to be rather human-like, but that there was no hard evidence to support its existence.

Realizing that the local villagers she had spoken to considered the creature to be very real indeed, and not at all unusual, Martyr went straight back to search for the Orang Pendek. She has been on the trail of the elusive animal ever since, visiting Sumatra when she can take time off from her work to do so. What is known of this cryptid is largely due to her work. In 1999, Debbie Martyr was rewarded for her persistence by a sighting of what she described as a 'bipedal half-ape, half-gibbon looking orang pendek'.

In 2003 two new researchers, Adam Davies and Andrew Sanderson, found hairs and made a cast of a footprint. These were sent to Cambridge University for study. Examination of the footprint cast revealed that it came from an ape that had features of both the human and chimpanzee foot, but that the cast matched no known primate. The hairs were studied by the Austrian specialist Dr Hans Brunner. He concluded that they were from a primate, but he could not assign them to any known species.

Then, in 2005, the National Geographic Society set up a project in the Mount Tenici region based on the use of camera traps. These are cameras that are operated when something moves within their field of vision. To date, however, nothing definitive has been photographed.

It seems that the Orang Pendek was formerly widely distributed over the rainforest-covered hills of southern Sumatra. The island covers almost 200,000 square miles and even today there are large stretches of virgin forest. However, the growth of the oil and timber industries has meant that there is an increasingly complex network of roads through the interior. Also, men are now hunting for sport or food, so they are pushing into many areas that were previously utterly remote. The Orang Pendek does not seem to welcome such an intrusion by human outsiders and is now reported from an increasingly smaller area. By the 1990s reported encounters were coming only from an area between Bangko and Mount Kerinici. This is a stretch of untouched rainforest many hundreds of square miles in extent. It is big, but nowhere near as large as the area of forest that is no longer untouched.

The Orang Pendek is said by those who have seen it to look like a short human – hence its name – though with some clear differences. For a start it has a light covering of dark fur that is thicker on the limbs than on the body. The top of the head carries a mane of much longer hair that grows down the back at least as far as the shoulder blades and perhaps to the waist. Its forehead is high and its ears are like those of a human while the body is stocky and muscular, with a prominent pot-belly. Coming to the limbs, its arms are a bit longer than those of a human, but not so elongated as are those of the gibbons and its legs are like those of a human. The creature walks on its hind legs alone and the few footprints that have been found and cast in plaster show that its foot is very like that of a human. In fact, it has an arch and five toes arranged along the front edge. In size the footprints are about the same as those made by a 7- or 8-year-old human child, but rather wider at the front and with a very robust ball joint behind the big toe.

Dawn and dusk are the times at which the creatures seem to be active, at least that is when they are seen raiding the fields for sugar cane, bananas and other food crops. The creatures are usually seen alone, though sometimes a mother and her young will be in the same group. Only very rarely are two adults seen together. However, when one of them calls they are sometimes answered by another creature that is hidden in the undergrowth and tree foliage.

There the matter rests. There have been no official, or even semi-official, attempts to find the Orang Pendek. When Martyr tried to interest the Director of the Kerinici National Park, which covers 4 million acres of virgin rain forest, she was met by frank disbelief. He knew all about the stories, but did not believe them because the local people were 'simple and uneducated'.

10 The Australian Yowie

The Hairy Fellah

For many decades the wooded hills of eastern Australia have yielded reports of a creature that is sometimes called The Hairy Fellah. It is now more properly termed the Yowie, a word that grew out of just one of the many Aboriginal terms for this creature in New South Wales. Other words from the various Aboriginal languages include gulaga, thoolalgarl, doolagarl, myngawin and joogabinna.

Aboriginal stories about this creature are diverse and often feature elements of the supernatural. For instance, the Dulugars of the Suggan Buggan are not only inclined to kidnap human women for the purpose of mating with them, but they will do so by flying through the air. The Yalanji people have their own particular demon, the Quinkin, which they think is taller than a tree, while the Yaroma travel in pairs. Standing back to back and moving in a series of great leaps they have mouths so large that they can swallow men whole. Clearly these stories owe much to myth and folklore, but that does not mean that there is no basis of fact behind them.

Very few reports of Yowies, or similar creatures, came from the Aboriginal people before their areas were overrun by European settlers. When they did, a rather more mundane creature was involved. Black Harry, a leader of the Ngunnawal people, reported that in about 1847 he had seen a group of warriors attack and kill one of these creatures on the banks of the Murrumbidgee River. He said that the mystery creature was 'like a black man, but covered all over with grey hair'.

By the time European settlers were moving into Aborigine lands during the 19th century, the picture had got a bit confused. A hugely popular book of the time, *Gulliver's Travels*, talked about an entirely fictional race of hairy giant men called Yahoos who lived on an island in the Pacific. Some of the early settlers began to refer to the mysterious large hairy creature that was reported by the Aborigines as 'Yahoos'. They assumed that they were talking about hairy giants, even if the evidence did not support this.

A number of Europeans began to see the hairy creatures too. In 1848, W. Sutton reported that one of his shepherds had come across a 'hairy man' in the bush near Cudgegong, New South Wales (NSW). The man's dogs had run away from the creature, which had then wandered off. Eight years or so after that, in 1856, William Collin was camped near Port Hacking in New South Wales when he saw a 'wild man of the woods'. Then, in 1860, a Miss Derrincourt saw 'something in the shape of a very tall man, seemingly covered with a coat of hair ... a Yahoo or some such'.

There was another lone sighting in 1871 when George Osborne watched an ape-like creature climb down from a tree as he was riding through Bush near Avondale, NSW. But

Reports indicate that the Yowie is rather more human than some of its fellow cryptid humanoids.

The Harper sighting of 1912, which produced one of the most detailed early descriptions of the 'big hairy fellah'.

then, in 1876, no fewer than nine Europeans were on the Laachlan River when they saw, according to one of them:

'... an inhuman, unearthly looking being bearing in every way the shape of a man with a big red face, hands and legs covered with long shaggy hair. The head was covered with dark, grissly hair, the face with shaggy, dark hair, the back and belly with hair of a lighter colour. This devil-devil, or whatever it may be called, doubled round and fled.'

In 1882 a European gave the first clear description of this mysterious animal. H.J. McCooey came across a creature near Batemans Bay, NSW.

'My attention was attracted by the cries of a number of birds which were pursuing and darting at it. It was partly upright, looking up at the birds, blinking its eyes and making a chattering sound. The creature was nearly 5 feet [152 cm] tall and covered with very long black hair which was dirty red or snuff colour about the throat and breast. Its eyes, which were small and restless, were partly hidden by matted hair. The length of the arms seemed out of proportion. It would probably have weighed about 8 stone.'

McCooey threw a stone at it, and the creature ran off.

In 1912 Charles Harper was camping out on Currickbilly Ridge NSW with two companions when they heard a 'low rumbling growl' coming from the darkness. One of the men threw a handful of twigs on to the embers of the camp fire, causing flames to spring up and illuminate the creature that had been making the noise. Harper later recorded it as being 'a huge man-like animal growling, grimacing and thumping his breast with his huge, hand-like paws. I should say its height would be 5ft 8in to 5ft 10in. Its body, legs and arms were covered with long brownish-red hair which shook with every quivering movement of its body.

The hair on its shoulders and back parts appeared in the light of the fire to be jet black and long; but what struck me as most extraordinary was the apparently human shape, but still so very different. The body frame was enormous, indicating immense strength and power of endurance. The arms and forepaws were long and large, and very muscular being covered with shorter hair. The head and face were small but very human. The eyes were large, dark and piercing, deeply set. A most horrible mouth was ornamented with two large and long canine teeth. When the jaws were closed they protruded over the lower lip.' The creature stood watching the men for a few seconds, then dropped on to all fours and raced off in to the bush.

Thereafter the reports continued to arrive, but in less detailed fashion. Mr N. Hambly was near Wollongong, NSW, in 1930 when he saw 'a strange animal... a wild bear'. Just a year later, in 1931, a girl called Molly saw 'a huge man with a funny head and long hair'. Then, in 1933, Lola Irish was in the Megalong Valley of the Blue Mountains when she saw 'a giant, hairy ape-man'. A couple of years later stockman Joe Carroll was riding out near Kempsey, NSW, when he saw an odd creature.

'He was almost within 50 feet [15 m] when he saw this creature about 5 feet [152 cm] tall with long hair and heavily built with long arms. When the creature saw him he got up from a sitting position and walked away with a steady gait.'

On 7 August 1970 Rex Gilroy was resting in a bush area near Katoomba when he saw a hairy, human-like creature walk across a clearing only a few feet away from him. Gilroy then began looking into Yowie reports and soon became convinced that a species of giant ape-men lived in the Blue Mountains. He established a natural history museum and spent his time trying to prove his ideas. He sometimes made claims that could be disproved, but he did succeed in establishing the Yowie as a subject for serious research by others interested in cryptozoology. That, in turn, made people more willing to make reports about encounters with the Yowie.

> The creature stood up on its hind legs. Its front legs hung down in front, like those of a bear, but its feet were more like hands than paws. Huge muscled shoulders that sported long hair completed the picture.

So Billy Southwell was happy to come forward with his story in 1976. He was resting late one evening in his cabin near Lake George, NSW, when his dog began barking excitedly. Southwell opened the door and stepped on to the porch. Standing at the end of the verandah was an 'apey-like' creature, about 5 feet 8 inches (172 cm) tall. It was heavy set and muscular with ginger-brown hair about 2 inches (5 cm) long over its body. The creature turned and fled as soon as Southwell appeared.

A year later, in May 1977, Geoff Nelson was driving near Taree, NSW, when he saw a human-shaped beast well over 6 feet (182 cm) tall and covered in hair bound into the road from his right. It ran across the road and leapt over a fence to disappear into woodland. In August the same year John Croker was riding a motorbike along a road near Talbingo, NSW, when he saw in the woods a human-shaped, hair-covered figure that looked to be about 9 feet (273 cm) tall. He rode off at speed, but returned later with some companions.

The creature had gone, but there were broken twigs and brush to show that something large had been there.

Two years passed, then in April 1979 Mr and Mrs Leo George were bushwalking near Wentworth Falls, NSW, when they came across a dead kangaroo which had been partly eaten by some wild animal. Looking around they saw a shaggy grey creature around 10 feet (304 cm) tall moving off into the bush. A couple of years after that, in May 1981, three teenage boys were walking near Dunoon when they saw two man-like creatures covered in dense hair walking ahead of them along a track. The boys saw one of the creatures seem to stumble, then glance round and see them. Both creatures then took off at speed. George Paras saw the head of a creature peering out of some bushes in February 1984. It was about 5 feet (152 cm) tall and it looked human-like. The head was covered in coarse brown hair, with very long hair on top that was swept back.

'Giant Wombat'

Then, in 1987, came a very clear sighting at close range. Stan Pappin was felling trees near Goothie, Queensland, when he heard a large animal approaching. When the creature emerged from the undergrowth it was about 18 feet (5.5 m) away. The beast looked very much like a big bear, but with a human-like head. Its muzzle was very short and the ears were human-like. It had a rather snub nose which was clearly defined and free of hair, while its chin was receding. A very stocky and muscular neck joined its head to its body. The creature had approached on all fours, but it now stood up on its hind legs. It could be seen that its front legs hung down in front, like those of a bear, but its feet were more like hands than paws. Huge muscled shoulders that sported long hair completed the picture. After regarding Pappin for a few seconds, the creature turned, took a few steps then dropped down on all fours and ran off at speed.

The report was strangely reminiscent of a report from Braidwood made in 1893. This concerned a 'giant wombat' that had been killed by Arthur Martin on 28 October and carried into Braidwood. The animal had a weight of 7 stone and its tailless body measured 4 feet (122 cm) from head to rump. Its head was like that of a bear, but shorter and it was covered with stout hair of a pale brown colour. The four legs were slender and ended in feet that looked like the hands of a man with overgrown fingernails. This creature had also approached on all fours, then stood up on its hind legs when it got close to Martin.

Other than their size the creatures killed by Martin and seen by Pappin are not too dissimilar to the normal 3-foot-long (91 cm) or so wombats that are seen everywhere. Also, fossils of enormous wombat-like creatures have been found in southeastern Australia. The Diprotodon was about 10 feet (304 cm) long and it died out only about 15,000 years ago.

It is not beyond the realms of possibility that a large type of wombat might have survived in remote areas.

That raises the question of exactly what the Yowie is. Perhaps influenced by reports of the Sasquatch, modern researchers and witnesses have tended to emphasize the animal's supposed ape-like characteristics. However not all of the witnesses actually report an ape-like creature. Something more like a giant wombat would fit the descriptions just as well in some cases, especially if it were to be capable of standing and taking a few steps on its hind legs.

In 2004, for instance, Margo Braithwaite saw a very tall, dark figure standing motionless in scrub near her home. She could see only the silhouette because it was a dark, rainy day, and the figure disappeared when she went to get her shoes on to investigate. However, by measuring a tree beside which the creature had been standing she estimated it to be about 7 feet (213 cm) tall.

Other reports indicate a creature that is definitely more ape or human in appearance. For instance, in August 2001 Mrs Laidley was driving near Mulgowies, Queensland, when she saw an 'orangutan-like animal with a bare bottom' cross the road. It was, she said, about as big as an Alsatian dog.

Not too long afterwards, in April 2003, Jason Cole saw a gorilla-like creature staring at him from nearby undergrowth while he was felling trees near Ormeau, Queensland. When he looked at it, the creature slipped out of sight but Cole could hear it moving about for some time. Then in May of the same year Drew Frost came across a 'hairy ape' while walking in the Blue Mountains. He fled.

Crashing of foliage

A few years later, in February 2006, a man living near Cessnock saw a huge human-shaped figure. It was about 8 feet (244 cm) tall and it was walking with long strides across a patch of grass some 30 yards away.

In January 2004 Paul Compton was camping out with his father-in-law near Glen Innes, NSW. They were beside a river and had bedded down for the night when they heard the sound of animals crashing through the bush coming from the far bank. This was followed by a loud splash, then more crashing of foliage. Paul grabbed a torch and shone it across the river. The beam revealed a grey kangaroo in the stream, having leapt into it, while a second kangaroo on the far bank was leaping about in circles as if very frightened. At the limit of the torch beam could be seen the reason for the fear of the two kangaroos – a hairy ape-like figure standing upright on its two hind legs. The beast was about 6 feet tall. After staring at the torch for a few seconds, the beast turned and fled.

The Yowie, seen in the summer of 2004 near Glen Innes, appeared to be chasing a young kangaroo.

What is striking about the Yowie reports that feature an ape- or human-like creature is that the sightings are generally in poor light or last for only a few seconds. Under such circumstances it is remarkably easy for a person to be mistaken, especially if they have already heard about the possible existence of a cryptid such as the Yowie.

A 1987 Yowie case makes the point about the unreliability of eyewitness accounts with startling clarity. On 22 February the *Brisbane Mail* carried a report of a Yowie sighting. Frank Burns, Phyllis Kenny and Mrs Kenny's four grandchildren were motoring across the outback near Alice Springs when they stopped at a waterhole for a rest. Mr Burns lit a fire and began brewing up a cup of tea while Mrs Kenny got out a picnic lunch and the children ran about playing games. Suddenly a terrifying figure leapt out of a large, open-topped water storage tank. Mrs Kenny later described the figure as:

'... a man-like animal covered with hair and standing at least 2 metres [6 feet 6 inches] tall. You can tell the difference between a man and a beast, and that was no man. There are some things that you just can't explain, that are just scary, and that was one of them. I nearly died.'

One of the older children said:

'It ran like a gorilla. Its arms hung down at its sides and it just sort of loped along. It had big eyes, a large forehead and it was all red around the mouth.'

The family fled to their vehicle and drove off at speed. The last they saw was the 'Yowie' trying to grab the back of their vehicle. They reported the matter to the police, then to the press.

A few weeks later the newspapers published a follow up report from the police. Two patrolmen were sent out to investigate and found the 'Yowie' sitting by the side of the road. He turned out to be a completely human man well known to locals. Franjo Jurcevic was a Yugoslav immigrant who had taken to living wild in the area some years earlier. He survived by eating wild foods, eked out by alcohol and food bought at a local store with his social welfare money.

'He never talks to anyone when he comes in,' the store owner told the press. 'He just takes his beer, whisky, fruit and veggies, pays and off he goes.'

The press described Mr Jurcevic as 'a desert hermit standing 6 foot 8 inches [202 cm] tall and 20 stone. He has hair everywhere and wears shorts and shirt, but sometimes goes naked.'

THE HAIRY FELLAH

No doubt the desert hermit, who had presumably been bathing naked in the water tank, cut an alarming figure. Mrs Kenny and her family were startled and frightened, especially when the apparition began walking towards them. They then leapt to the conclusion that what they were seeing was a ferocious Yowie creature, so they fled. Interestingly enough, though, the descriptions they later gave of the Yowie fitted Mr Jurcevic quite well. He was indeed 'a man-like animal covered with hair and standing at least 2 metres tall', and he 'had big eyes, a large forehead and... was all red around the mouth.'

What this incident proves is that people can be very easily mistaken in their conclusions and the interpretation of what they see. But this does not necessarily mean that the entire incident is worthless. Unfortunately the majority of Yowie witnesses do not manage to get close to the creature in good visibility. When they do, the sighting can be explained by creatures much more mundane than a cryptid ape or a primitive human. The creatures seen by Stan Pappin, Arthur Martin and others could easily have been very large wombats. We know that such creatures were relatively numerous until only a few thousand years ago, so it is quite possible that small numbers of them have managed to survive in the more remote regions.

The sightings of early European settlers, since included in Yowie literature, may have been of more interest to an anthropologist than a zoologist. These early sightings tend to speak of a 'hairy man' or a 'wild man of the woods' or 'something in the shape of a very tall man, seemingly covered with a coat of hair'. The most obvious explanation is that these people did, in fact, see a hairy man.

We know that Aborigines can have as much body hair as Europeans, so a very hairy male with long hair and a beard might appear rather odd if seen suddenly. We also know that some Aboriginal tribes imposed exile on malefactors or forced individuals to undertake rituals that might take them away from the tribe for weeks or months on end. Some Aborigines formed tiny religious groups that practised rites that are now forgotten, some of them involving violence on their fellow humans. All these might account for hairy Aborigines behaving in an odd manner. None of this necessarily proves that the Yowie does not exist. The old Aboriginal tales of flying hairy hominids and the modern eyewitness accounts might be based on the existence of a very real ape-like creature or perhaps a giant wombat.

No doubt the desert hermit, who had presumably been bathing naked in the water tank, cut an alarming figure. Mrs Kenny and her family were startled and frightened...

197

YOWIE   ORANG PENDEK   YEREN

YETI   MARICOXI   WILDMAN

Conclusion

In Medieval times, 'wild men' or 'woodwoses' were reported in Europe's dense forests. These two figures come from a painting of 1499.

Throughout this book, I have tried to present the evidence for the existence of man-like apes around the world in as impartial a manner as possible. Unsurprisingly, the evidence has been interpreted in different ways by sceptics and believers, but I have sought to give both sides an equal hearing.

None of the creatures that I have featured has been accepted by the wider scientific community, though some individual scientists have stated their conviction that one or more of these beasts is real. Others have stated their willingness to look at the evidence, which is a start. Perhaps the most important hindrance to proving that any cryptid exists is the quality of the evidence. Quantity is not a problem, because there have been quite literally thousands of reports of cryptid apes from around the world. It is the credibility of those reports that is in question.

Footprints can be faked, films can be hoaxed and nests can be built by human hands. Not only can these things happen but we know that they have taken place.

Frauds and hoaxes of many different types have been exposed over the years. This is all that a sceptic needs to be able to cast doubt on all of the 'evidence'.

The most controversial, and at the same time the most common, type of evidence is sightings of cryptid animals by humans. For some of the cryptids, such as the Almas or the Maricoxi, eyewitness accounts are pretty much the only evidence available. Again frauds and hoaxes are not only possible but are known to have occurred. But even when in all honesty a person reports having seen a cryptid, it does not necessarily mean that they have seen an unknown animal. People can easily be mistaken in what they see, especially if lighting conditions are poor and the creature is seen only fleetingly.

There comes a time, however, when the author of a book such as this has to nail his colours to the mast, give his opinion of the evidence and suggest what should be done about it. It does no good simply to report the evidence but then avoid making any firm judgements on the subject. So here, for what it is worth, is what I think.

I believe that there is a Sasquatch living in the forested mountains of northwestern

North America. And I believe that it corresponds to the figure seen in the Patterson movie. The evidence for its existence falls short of proof, but the balance of probabilities would suggest that there is such a creature. I think that it is probably confined to that area of the continent, though it was probably distributed much more widely until the arrival of the Europeans with their more intensive farming techniques.

I do not think that the evidence supports the survival of the Sasquatch outside the western forests. Nor do I believe that the Skunk Ape is a real, living animal. The evidence for its existence is weak and largely circumstantial. I do not, however, rule it out completely and would be pleased to be proved wrong should more evidence turn up.

I believe that there is a Sasquatch living in the forested mountains of northwestern North America.

Moving on to South America, the reports of the Maricoxi would seem to be descriptions of a type of human that is quite distinct from ourselves. We know that human evolution has produced many side branches, dead ends and detours. There is nothing intrinsically impossible about a distinct subspecies or species of human surviving to the present day. The evidence for it is, however, slim. Such evidence as there is relates back to a time when the vast forests of South America were utterly unexplored. These days, what with logging and forest clearance, there are few areas that are unknown. There is today no such tribe as the Maricoxi and all reports of primitive humans ceased some 30 years ago. The evidence would indicate that there are no tribes of early humans in South America and that most of the reports and stories could be dismissed as folktales and myth.

But then there is the report made by Colonel Percy Fawcett. Fawcett was very definite about what he had seen and experienced. He was a serious explorer who has never been found to have lied or to have misreported what he discovered – though he admittedly had some rather odd theories to account for it all. I think we must accept that Fawcett really did meet a tribe of hairy humans of rather primitive aspect, but we must also accept that whatever these humans were they are now extinct.

As for the Mono Grande, or whatever name is given to the giant monkey or small ape of northern South America, the evidence is quite beyond dispute. The existence of this creature is, I believe, quite beyond dispute, because there is a primate living in the dense forests that grows to be about 5 feet (152 cm) tall. Personally I would credit de Loys with accurately reporting the lack of a tail. However, I don't think that this necessarily makes the creature an ape. It may be a form of monkey that has evolved to be very large and which has adapted to a life on the ground. Such a creature may very well evolve in such a way that it loses its tail. So far as I can see, the problem with this creature is not whether or not it exists, but what it is. Hopefully a specimen will be brought in one day that will clarify the issue.

The primitive humans of Asia – the Yeren, the Almas and others – are a different proposition. Eyewitness reports are the only source of evidence and the regions in which they are said to live are remote and difficult to access. There are no footprint casts, no photographs and no hair samples, or at least none that have survived the recurrent political upheavals in those areas. However, the eyewitness evidence that has been collected is strong and consistent. Traditional folklore, reports from local tribesmen and sightings by Western observers all point towards some form of primitive human living in the forested mountains. The Neanderthal has been put forward as one solution to the mystery, but early human evolution in Asia is poorly understood so there might be some other subspecies to explain the reports.

If the various eyewitness accounts can be trusted then there can be no doubt that the Caucasus and the Tien Shan and Pamir mountain ranges do support small populations of a primitive type of human. However, all reports also agree that the creatures are being seen less often and across smaller territories. If they do exist, they are dying out. Personally, I find the evidence strong, but not convincing. Given the difficulty and the high cost of reaching these regions it is unlikely that much new evidence is going to be found at any time soon.

> The Yeti is a real puzzle. Taken at face value the evidence produced for its existence is meagre indeed. Footprints have been found, but the evidence they provide is inconclusive.

The Yeti is a real puzzle. Taken at face value the evidence produced for its existence is meagre indeed. Footprints have been found, but the evidence they provide is inconclusive. Also, the sightings by Europeans are so rare as to be meaningless and the few supposed remains have turned out to be from other animals. However, the habits ascribed to the beast and the overall description of it could easily fit a bear. In fact, common sense would indicate that the Yeti is nothing more than a bear. Seen in difficult light and by a person thinking about the Yeti, a bear could easily be taken for something else.

And yet... And yet... The people who inhabit the Himalayas are absolutely convinced that the Yeti is a real animal and they consistently describe it as being a large ape. This in a place where, so far as is known, apes have not lived for hundreds of thousands of years. How would farmers and herdsmen living in remote mountain valleys come up with a description of an ape if the nearest apes lived thousands of miles away across half a continent of mountains, forests and hostile kingdoms? It would be much easier to believe that they described an ape-like creature because they had seen one.

In the final analysis I am unconvinced by the Yeti, but I do not rule it out completely. I think that there may be an ape up in the mountain forests but I consider it rather unlikely.

The Orang Pendek fits into a similar category to the Yeti. The evidence is thin, but curiously persuasive, because the local people are quite clearly convinced that it is a real animal that shares their forests with them. It is treated by them as a flesh and blood animal, not some sort of supernatural being. Stories from these farmers and hunters are many and they consistently describe a diminutive human-like creature that is neither ape nor monkey. Reports by outsiders are much rarer, and one of those was almost certainly a sighting of an unusually large gibbon. Hard evidence is very scarce and inconclusive.

On the face of it the evidence for the Orang Pendek is thin to the point of vanishing. And yet the locals seem to be quite definite on the subject. Moreover, the pattern of the reports is not only credible but indicative of a real creature. In the early 20th century the Orang Pendek was reported from a wide range that ran across southern Sumatra and it was always seen in remote and effectively unexplored areas of upland forest. Today the creature is still reported from remote forested hills, but since the area that remains unfrequented by outsiders has shrunk greatly so has the area from which reports are made. This is exactly what would be expected of sightings of a shy creature that prefers to avoid humans. I would like to believe that the Orang Pendek does exist, but I cannot in all honesty rate the chances of this being the case at much over 50 per cent.

Space to hide

The case for the Yowie is even thinner. Aboriginal beliefs from pre-settlement times were recorded only sporadically by Europeans. In some cases they have clearly been influenced by the person writing them down. Reports from the 19th and early 20th century could easily be accounted for by sightings of Aborigines, particularly of those engaged on ritual journeys and tasks of various kinds. Aborigines can be tall and they can be hairy. More recent accounts are often just as vague as the older ones and, at least since the 1960s, have been given by people who are familiar with the story of a 'hairy fellah' living in the bush. There is a lot of evidence, but nearly all of it is based on eyewitness testimony, not on footprints, hair samples or other hard data.

Nor is the theory behind the Yowie very convincing. The continent of Australia was isolated for millions of years. Apart from the ancestors of native marsupials and reptiles, the only creatures that have arrived from outside since the isolation have been those that could fly or travel on a boat. There is no evidence that any very early forms of humans ever built boats capable of a sea crossing. It is highly unlikely, therefore, that any ape or lower form of human made it to Australia before the ancestors of the Aborigines.

I don't really think that the Yowie can be the unknown cryptid that its supporters suggest. The evidence for a species of upright-walking hairy ape simply does not stack up. That said, Australia is a vast country and there is plenty of space for things to hide.

If anyone is any doubt that it is possible for a large creature to hide in unfrequented areas without being found by humans, they should look at the case of the Yahi, a First Nation of North America that lived in the Sierra Nevadas of California. The 1,400 or so Yahi lived a hunter-gatherer lifestyle and were but one of several tribes of the larger Yana group of the region. However, in 1848 they had the great misfortune to have gold found on their territory.

White gold miners flooded into the area and violent clashes with the Yahi led to a bloodbath. The fighting culminated in the Three Knolls Massacre of 1865 when a large group of miners surrounded the last Yahi village and launched a dawn attack. Men, women and children were all killed and by the end of the day the miners were convinced that they had wiped out the entire Yahi people.

However, a group of about 30 Yahi had not been in camp at the time. They found the bodies of their tribesmen and held a meeting to discuss what to do. They decided to take to the forests, avoid all white men and seek to survive until the gold had run out and the miners had gone. At Oroville on 29 August 1911 the Yahi re-emerged into history when the last survivor was caught apparently trying to filch food. For the previous 46 years the tribe had managed to survive, though with ever dwindling numbers, in the Sierra Nevada without once attracting the attention of the thousands of Americans who lived in the area.

This photo taken by Eric Shipton (1951) in the Himalayas shows that whatever left these tracks walked on two feet.

Clearly it is possible to evade humans for a long time, even in fairly well-known and well-travelled regions.

Over the years a vast amount of evidence has been collected about the Sasquatch, the Orang Pendek, the Almas and other cryptid apes. And yet none of them has yet been accepted as a real animal by the scientific establishment. I have outlined some of the problems: the types of evidence produced; the funding system for scientific research; and the career paths of scientists. In my view none of these cryptids will be accepted as a genuine creature until somebody hauls a body out of the wilderness. Understandably, given that these creatures seem to be becoming rarer, many researchers do not want to do that. They continue to bombard scientists with eyewitness reports, footprint casts and photographs, but get nowhere.

Different path

Some researchers are beginning to think that a different path should be taken. Rather than try to convince the scientists, it has been suggested that efforts should be made to convince the politicians. After all, politicians control the purse strings of a nation.

If they are convinced that a creature exists they are able to fund scientific research and massive hunts and they have the authority to deploy all sorts of high tech equipment. The United States military operates drone aircraft carrying infra-red equipment designed to find and identify a single human terrorist in the vast wilds of Afghanistan. Deploying such equipment is fiendishly expensive, but if one such drone were sent up over the Bluff Creek area it surely would not take long to establish the existence or otherwise of Sasquatch.

It has been suggested that some sort of official inquiry would be the best start. The hope is that a group of politicians could be persuaded to launch an investigation. Ideally such an investigation would take an unbiased look at the existing evidence and then reach a decision on the balance of probabilities. Such an inquiry would no doubt gain the support and co-operation of the researchers and eyewitnesses. If that inquiry came to the conclusion that the evidence indicated that there was a real creature behind the reports, then that might be enough to unlock the government coffers to fund some proper, large-scale research that might actually prove that such creatures exist.

> Men, women and children were all killed and by the end of the day the miners were convinced that they had wiped out the entire Yahi people.

Save the Sasquatch

The best chance of success is offered by a study of the Sasquatch in the Western United States and Canada. There are various reasons for this: both the United States and Canada are relatively wealthy nations; the supposed home of the Sasquatch is not as remote as, say, the Tien Shan mountains; and the evidence for the Sasquatch is relatively strong.

If the evidence relating to the Sasquatch is to be taken at anything like face value then its range and numbers have declined dramatically in the past 200 years. And things are getting worse.

René Dahinden has commented that when he began looking for the Sasquatch almost 50 years ago footprints and other signs were found with great regularity in areas even fairly close to human habitation. Now he has to push higher and higher in the mountains or deeper into unfrequented forests to find less evidence than before. If Sasquatch is not proved to exist soon, it might be too late.

It would be a great crime if science did not accept the reality of the Sasquatch until after it was extinct.

INDEX

PICTURE CREDITS